The House of Lords UFO Debate.

©Crown Copyright text of the debate
reproduced by permission of *Hansard*.
UFO photograph kindly supplied by the
Aetherius Society where founder Dr. George
King, claims many UFO contacts, one of
which provided the specifications for this
model.
This edition first published 1979 by
Open Head Press, 2 Blenheim Crescent,
London W11 1NN in association with
Pentacle Books, 6 Perry Road, Bristol 1.

ISBN0 9506772 0 5

Printed by *Castle Camelot Printers*, Bristol

The House of Lords UFO Debate.
Illustrated, Full Transcript with Preface
by Lord Clancarty (Brinsley le Poer Trench)
and Notes by John Michell.

OPEN HEAD PRESS\PENTACLE BOOKS

The House of Lords, the upper chamber of
the British Parliament, is made up of the two
Archbishops and 24 Senior English Bishops
(Lords Spiritual), and peers of hereditary
title or life peers, together with Law Lords
(Lords Temporal).

Preface.

It might be appropriate if before coming to discuss the UFO Debate that I introduced in the House of Lords I gave some indication as to how UFOs became one of my big interests. Actually, I have been involved with this absorbing subject for over thirty years, that is pretty well since the end of World War II.

Soon after the War there were quite a lot of sighting reports of these mysterious objects in the press, and I started keeping a scrap book, putting in news cuttings about the flying saucers, as they were generally called in those days.

Then, I met Desmond Leslie who had co-authored a book called 'Flying Saucers have Landed', with George Adamski, a well known con-tactee who died from a heart attack a few years back.

Desmond invited me to hear him talk about the flying saucers at the Battersea Polytechnic. So I went along and met some other friends of his, including Derek Dempster, who was then aviation correspondent on the 'Daily Express'. Eventually, I met up with about ten people, and we all decided to put in ten pounds each towards buying shares to form a company called Flying Saucer Service Ltd, which would enable us to publish a magazine called 'Flying Saucer Review'. Well, the first issue was published in the Spring of 1955. It was at first intended to be quarterly, but after the first issue it became bi-monthly. The original Editor was Derek Dempster that I mentioned earlier. In September 1956, I took over as Editor until September 1959, when I handed over to Waveney Girvan, the publisher of Desmond Leslie and George Adamski's book. He remained Editor until his untimely death. For the last fourteen years Charles Bowen has ably edited the magazine, and it is now coming up for its 25th year of publication.

Incidentally, I have now succeeded in getting 'Flying Saucer Review' into the House of Lords Library!

After I resigned as Editor of the magazine, I started to write books about the mysterious flying objects. I have now written seven books under my actual name, Brinsley Le Poer Trench, most of them have gone into American and foreign editions. Indeed, four are now in Japanese.

In 1967 I started Contact International, a world-wide UFO movement which has some 37 member countries. I am no longer running it, but am referred to as Founder President. I am happy to report that we have a very nice woman, Miss Ruth Rees, as our President. She is a splendid person and doing a great job.

Now, at this stage I should tell you why I put my motion down for debate in the House of Lords. I had been informed that the sighting figures reaching the Data Research Division of Contact International were very much on the increase. About a year ago the sighting reports coming to us from all over the world were running at around 300 to 400 a month. Now they are coming in at the rate of over a thousand a month. I was worried that this very large increase in UFO sightings might be the introduction to open landings by UFOs, and if that happened here there might well be panic, as the authorities have not prepared the public for such an event at all. So I decided to put a motion down for debate and try to get the Government to take some action.

It will always remain in my mind as a memorable occasion when I introduced the Debate on UFOs on the 18th January, this year (1979), in the House of Lords. A unique occasion indeed, and the first time in the 700 years' history of that prestigious place that the UFOs had been debated there.

What pleased me about the Debate was that the subject was taken seriously and not ridiculed. Those who held views either for or against UFOs expressed them most seriously.

For about four weeks prior to the Debate a big TV, radio and press campaign was in action. I was interviewed on three TV programmes. By the time the great day arrived public interest was very high. I should mention that some films, especially 'Close Encounters of the Third Kind' have contributed to the growing public interest in UFOs. Indeed, the public's interest can be confirmed by the fact that during the Debate the Public Gallery was jam-packed.

Before putting down my motion for the Debate I had done some lobbying among my fellow Peers to see who was interested in taking part. To my surprise I found quite a number, and in fact, there were some fourteen speakers in the Debate.

As you will see, reading this book about the Debate, many distinguished people took part. Amongst those that supported me were the Earl of Kimberley, the Liberal Party spokesman on aerospace; a Scottish Peer, Lord Rankeillour, who had read one of my books; Lord Gainford, who stated in his speech that he, along with other witnesses, including some children, had seen a UFO; a Welsh Peer, Lord Davies of Leek, who was from the Labour benches; the Earl of Cork and Orrery, and Lord Gladwyn.

Those who opposed were two Conservative Peers, Lord Trefgarne and Lord Hewlett, as well as Lord Strabolgi, who replied for the Government.

Two very distinguished scientists spoke in the Debate. These were Lord Kings Norton, who used to be President of the Royal Institution, as well as being connected with the early airships; and Lord Halsbury who has been a member of many scientific committees and organisations.

This was my motion − To call attention to the increasing number of sightings on a world-wide scale of unidenitifed flying objects (UFOs) and to the need for an intra-governmental study of UFOs: and to move for papers. I originally put it down asking for an inter-governmental study but it got altered to intra-governmental study which is something quite different!

It is curious, as you will see, that in my opening speech I mentioned a number of UFO sightings in November 1975, at U.S. Strategic Air Command bases in Michigan, Montana, North Dakota and Maine, over a 13 day period. Several UFOs were hovering over nuclear weapons storage areas. When interceptor planes were sent up to investigate, the UFOs dimmed their lights and became invisible.

Two days after the Debate, the 'Daily Mail' published on the 20th January, a news item from their Washington correspondent, Simon King. It stated that the Pentagon had always averred that there was nothing to all these UFO reports. There was nothing to it at all.

Yet, you see, for a long time they had been collecting hundreds of secret files on UFO sightings! The Pentagon had to admit that UFOs had been seen over those nuclear weapons storage areas at those strategic Air Command bases I mentioned in my speech. You see, there is now a Freedom of Information Act in the U.S.A., which allows individuals and organisations to take legal action against government departments in order to get information released to them, providing that it does not affect national security.

Anyway, 900 pages of official records about UFOs were released from the Pentagon files as a result of an action brought by a civilian UFO organisation, the Ground Saucer Watch, of Phoenix, Arizona. These records show that government experts were unable to explain the large number of sightings over those nuclear storage areas in November 1975.

I knew that Ground Saucer Watch was bringing a case to obtain some information, but did not realise that it concerned those particular sightings I mentioned in the Debate. So, it was quite extraordinary that these were highlighted two days later.

In my speech in the Debate I mentioned that in February, 1974, the then French Minister of Defence, Monsieur Robert Galley, was interviewed entirely about UFOs on France-Inter radio station. Monsieur Galley stated that UFOs existed but freely admitted he did not know all the answers. He said that the Gendarmerie were taking part in investigating sightings and landings, as well as questioning witnesses and examining burnt circle marks on the ground. He also stated that there had been a unit in the French Ministry of Defence since 1954 collecting UFO reports. Some of these reports were sent down to the National Centre for Space Studies in Toulouse which is the French equivalent of the American NASA. There is a unit in the centre scientifically investigating UFO reports under a distinguished scientist, Monsieur Claud Poher, who was one of the designers of Concorde. I found out by putting down a question for written answer in the House of Lords that this unit is under French Government sponsorship, and comes under the French Ministry for Industry, Commerce and Artisans.

Monsieur Galley spoke quite openly to the French people about the UFOs in his radio interview, and they did not all run like lemmings into the sea. In the Debate I asked whether our Minister of Defence could give a TV interview and tell us what he knows about the UFOs.

I also suggested that from now on we should keep the UFO subject permanently in front of Parliament, and one way to do that would be to form a House of Lords UFO Study Group to meet about once a month.

I did not succeed in getting our Minister of Defence to talk about UFOs on TV, but since the Debate a number of Peers have indicated their wish to join a House of Lords UFO Study Group, so we are definitely going ahead with that project.

Finally, to add emphasis to the public interest, the day after the Debate more Peers than usual called at the Printed Paper Office in the House of Lords to ask for copies of Hansard containing the Debate. The Printed Paper Office ran out of copies. Normally, when that happens they order some more copies from H.M. Stationery Office in High Holborn. Well, that is what they did. However, no luck. H.M. Stationery Office had sold right out. You see, members of the Public had bought them all up! This was an unprecedented event to set the seal on a most unique and historic Debate.

Earl of Clancarty

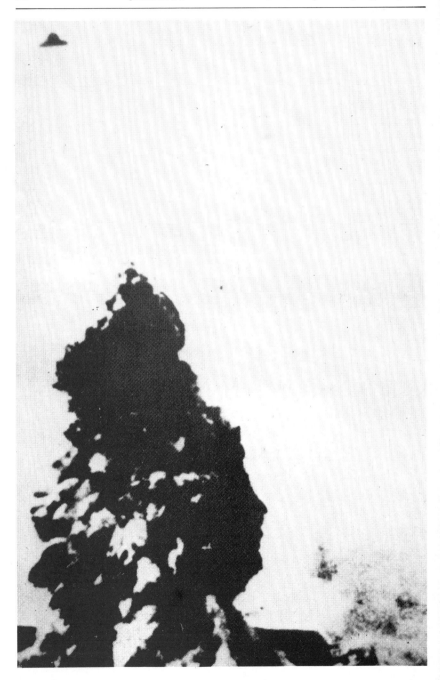

7.7 p.m.

The Earl of CLANCARTY rose to call attention to the increasing number of sightings and landings on a world-wide scale of unidentified flying objects (UFOs), and to the need for an intra-governmental study of UFOs; and to move for Papers. The noble Earl said: It is with much pleasure that I introduce this debate this evening about unidentified flying objects—known more briefly as UFOs and sometimes as flying saucers. I understand that this is the first time the subject of UFOs has been debated in your Lordships' House, so that this is indeed a unique occasion. Before proceeding further I think I should declare an interest, in that I have written a number of books about UFOs. I am grateful to those noble Lords who are going to follow me in this debate and I am sure that it will be a most stimulating discussion.

Before speaking about the need for an intra-governmental study of UFOs, which is the basis of my Motion being debated today, I think it advisable to give your Lordships some background to this fascinating subject of UFOs. I shall briefly cover a little history, the classes of witnesses, the characteristics of UFOs and some important sightings, and then I shall deal with the vital subject of the attitude of governments to these important phenomena.

Although UFOs have come to the fore since the end of the last World War, there are reports of them all through history. Among the papers of the late Professor Alberto Tulli, former director of the Egyptian Museum at the Vatican, was found one of the earliest known records of a fleet of flying saucers. It

THE EARL OF CLANCARTY, 67, is the pioneer UFO writer, Brinsley Le Poer Trench, who first introduced many of the ideas current in UFO literature. His books are: *The Sky People*, 1960, *Men Among Mankind*, 1962, *Forgotten Heritage*, 1964, *The Flying Saucer Story*, 1966, *Operation Earth*, 1969, *The Eternal Subject*, 1973, and *Secret of the Ages*, 1974. He founded the UFO society, CONTACT INTERNATIONAL, and has been active in many organizations for UFO debate and research. He likes travel and walking, and lives with his wife in London.

A classic of UFO photography is this picture, (Argentine Navy copyright), taken by the official photographer of an Argentine warship, of a volcanic eruption on Deception Island in the Antarctic, 4 December 1967. The flying saucer-like object was only seen when the film was developed. It illustrates a well noted phenomenon, the frequent appearance of UFOs at times and places of earthquakes and volcanic disturbances.

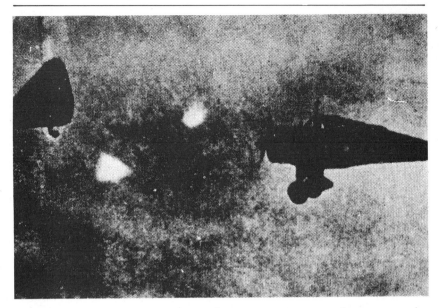

This photograph, taken during World War II shows the mysterious lights, called Foo Fighters, referred to here. Speculation by some pilots that they might come from space was an early example of the extra-terrestial theory applied to UFOs. The theory that they were prototypes of secret weapons or German anti-radar devices is still current in UFO literature.

was written on papryus long ago in ancient Egypt—actually, it was at the time of Thutmose III, circa 1504 to 1450 BC, who, with his army witnessed the sighting of what we today would call UFOs.

Now, I am not going to bore your Lordships with accounts of UFOs in every century because I want to get on to the very interesting things happening today. In modern times things began to happen during World War II when both allied and German pilots saw strange circular lights around their planes. We called them Foo fighters. Both Allied and German pilots thought that they were secret weapons of the other side. After the war, on 24th June 1947, an American called Kenneth Arnold, piloting his own plane, was on a mercy mission trying to find another aircraft that had crashed somewhere in the Cascade Mountains in the State of Washington. Suddenly, he spotted nine gleaming objects, crescent shaped, flying in a zigzag fashion between his plane and the mountains. He managed to calculate their speed because he was able to get a fix—I think that is the technical term—between two mountain peaks, Rainier and Baker. It appeared that the objects were travelling at some 1,400 miles per hour—a very fast speed in 1947.

The COMING of the SAUCERS

By Kenneth Arnold & Ray Palmer

For a full account of Kenneth Arnold's sighting, which produced the term 'flying saucers' in 1947, and for details of his and other people's UFO experiences at that time, see his book *The Coming of the Saucers,* co-authored with, and published by Ray Palmer, 1952.

Some time after landing, Arnold, in answer to a question from the Press, described the motion of the flying objects as being like saucers skimming over water. Next day the Press headlined them as " flying saucers ". Since Arnold's sighting in 1947, millions of people all over the world have seen the UFOs. This brings me to the class of witnesses that see UFOs. It is true that occasionally one gets the odd crank or hoaxer; but the majority of witnesses are sincere people. Then again many witnesses are pilots, police officers, coastguards, radar operators—in short, trained observers. Many astronauts have seen UFOs. Many people ask me: " Why is it that astronomers do not see them? " The answer is that they do. In a letter published in the *Daily Telegraph* on 4th January last year, I listed eight well-known astronomers who had seen UFOs, including Dr. Clyde Tombaugh, discoverer of the planet Pluto.

Now a few words, my Lords, about the UFOs themselves. Actually, the name " flying saucer " given by the Press in 1947 was a misnomer as they come in all sorts of shapes and sizes: cigar, oval, disc, sphere, doughnut, crescent and tadpole shaped. You name it, my Lords, the list is endless. I should like to say a few words about their characteristics.

Unexplained lights or luminous globes that travel along power cables or swoop on vehicles, causing temporary mechanical failure, are frequently reported but rarely photographed. This picture of a light ball which moved with a humming noise over high-tension wires at Cumana, Venezuela, and hovered for two or three minutes over a supporting tower was taken by a local government inspector of public projects.

UFOs often have very bright lights and sometimes when in flight change colours all the way through the colour spectrum. Sometimes the light from a UFO is so intense that its shape is obscured from view. This light energy is so powerful that witnesses have been burned on the face and hands if in too close a proximity to a UFO.

Another characteristic of the UFOs is electrical interference with various machines. UFOs have been notorious for stopping cars at short range. The driver will hear his engine splutter and it stops running. Besides cars, many other machines have been affected, including aircraft, motor cycles, buses, lorries and tractors. UFOs are said to be the cause of some of the power blackouts in the USA, Mexico and other countries. Indeed, UFOs have been seen flying along power lines in the USA just before black-outs. Furthermore, I have a picture on the wall of my study at home of a UFO doing just that!

Now, I will mention one or two of the more impressive sightings since the war. On the 29th June, 1954, a BOAC Boeing stratocruiser " Centaurus " had taken off from New York for London. Dinner had been served. The time was just after sunset when the skipper, Captain James Howard, first sighted the UFOs. Some of the passengers by then were asleep. There was one big object with six smaller ones. Captain Howard pointed them out to his co-pilot, First Officer Lee Boyd, who flew with the famous Pathfinder force in World War II. The objects were five miles from the " Centaurus ". They stayed parallel with the aircraft for

80 miles. From time to time the big object appeared to change shape. The radio officer checked with Goose Bay, Labrador, to see if any other aircraft were in the area and was told, No. Goose Bay sent a fighter up to investigate. All the crew saw the objects. Just before the fighter arrived, the objects began to disappear, and it seemed that the smaller ones went inside the large one. Altogether, a crew of eight and 14 of the 51 passengers saw the UFOs.

In November 1975, at Strategic Air Command Bases in Michigan, Montana, North Dakota and Maine, a number of UFOs were sighted over a 13 day period. Several were hovering near nuclear weapons storage areas. When interceptor planes were sent up to investigate, the UFOs dimmed their lights and became invisible. One of the most amazing UFO incidents ever occurred in Septembr, 1976. A report of this event written by Geoffrey Levy appeared in the *Daily Express* on 27th February, last year. I shall try and give you his account in my own words. A very large glowing object was seen over Teheran, Iran. Hundreds of witnesses telephoned the authorities. At 1.30 a.m. the Iranian Air Force scrambled a Phantom jet to investigate the UFO which was some 70 miles away. As the jet reached about half the distance to the UFO, all of the Iranian plane's communications and instrument systems malfunctioned. The pilot had no alternative but to return to base.

A second Phantom jet took off flying faster than the speed of sound. The UFO began to move at a very fast speed indeed, and soon outpaced the jet. Then, an extraordinary thing happened. Suddenly a second smaller UFO came out of the big one, and headed straight for the jet. The jet pilot tried to release an AIM-9 air-to-air missile at the glowing object. No success at all. The weapons control panel was not working and all electronic systems were out of action. There was only one thing for the pilot to do, and that was to make his escape. He put his plane in to a dive. Then something extraordinary happened. The second UFO turned around and went back inside the " mother ship ". The jet pilot's instruments started working again. So once more he tried to pursue the UFO, but it moved away too rapidly, and so the Phantom jet returned to base.

There are literally vast numbers of these astounding reports. Indeed, my Lords, this worldwide UFO invasion of every country's air space is of growing importance and therefore I suggest that Parliament keeps a continuous watch on the situation. I have thought of one way of doing this. In the same way that there is a House of Lords Defence Study Group ably chaired by the noble Lord, Lord Shinwell, perhaps we could have a House of Lords UFO Study Group to meet periodically. If any of your Lordships are interested, please let me know!

I should like to touch on the attitudes of Governments towards this subject and to stress the need for an intra-governmental study, which is the object of my Motion. I am only going to talk about four Governments, your Lordships will probably be pleased to know. First, let us take a look at the United States. I think that one of the reasons for " playing down " UFOs some years ago in the United States was the fear of panic among the public. This was partly based on an actual panic that did occur in 1938 due to a very realistic broadcast by Orson Welles of H. G. Wells' *War of the Worlds*. Thousands of people left their homes.

However, after the war, the United States Air Force investigated pilots' reports without any debunking. Then the Central Intelligence Agency, the CIA, stepped in. The CIA controls the intelligence departments of the United States military services. They ordered the United States Air Force to clamp down on UFO reports. That was, I believe in 1953 and it has been going on ever since. Pilots who reported seeing UFOs were ridiculed, and after a time other pilots did not report them for fear of damaging their reputation. We had high hopes during President Carter's election campaign that there was a strong possibility of a breakthrough to the truth about UFOs. He disclosed during his campaign that he had seen a UFO a few years previously in Georgia, and he added that if he got into the White House he would release to the public all the UFO information in the Pentagon. Unfortunately, that election pledge has not been fulfilled.

What has been happening in the Soviet Union? Probably the leading ufologist in that country is Doctor Felix Zigel, Professor of Higher Mathematics and Astronomy at the Moscow Aeronautical Institute. For a long time he had been trying to form a big UFO research group on a worldwide scale. Many UFOs have been seen over the Soviet Union. In July, August, September and October 1967, for instance, giant space ships were seen over various parts of the USSR by astronomers

President Carter's UFO sighting occured in 1973 during a 12-week period when thousands of people, including many members of police departments, were daily reporting UFOs over Georgia, the state of which Carter was then Governor. During his presidential campaign Carter publicly described the UFO which he had seen in company with 12 other witnesses. It was an intensely brilliant light which changed colour, hovering silently for ten minutes at a height of about 300 feet and then executed various manoeuvres, descending to roof-top height before moving away.

No doubt aware of the surveys which show that the majority of Americans believe in the reality of the UFO phenomenon, Carter stated that he took the matter seriously and he promised that, if elected, he would open the official secret files on UFOs. Since Carter's election, many reports and documents on the UFO problem have in fact been made public.

Carter's sighting has been 'explained' as the planet Venus, a suggestion which is repeated as if it were proven fact by Lord Hewlett later in this debate. Answers given to this are that Carter is a trained scientist and a former naval commander, used to navigating by the stars. He might therefore be trusted to recognize Venus, which in any case does not move rapidly in different directions about the sky.

Dr. Felix Zigel is known for his debunking of the official theory that the mysterious explosion in Siberia in 1908 was caused by a comet. In December 1967 he contributed an article to the magazine *Sputnik* about recent UFO sightings over Russia, stating that they were causing concern to the authorities, and a chapter by him on the same subject was included in *The Inhabited Cosmos*, a book published by *Science Press,* in Moscow, in which a number of scientists speculate on the possibility of intelligent life elsewhere in the universe. During his appearance on Russian television, together with Stoliarov, President of the Cosmonaut Committee, Zigel showed photographs and diagrams of UFOs seen over the Soviet Union, and appealed for unprejudiced, scientific research into the UFO problem. At that time the America committee which later produced the *Condon Report* on UFOs was meeting in Colorado, and a review of the Stoliarov-Zigel television programme was published prominently in the *New York Times* as evidence that the Russians were engaged in the same type of official UFO research as the Americans. This undignified publicity, as they regarded it, enraged the Soviet scientific establishment. Denials were issued of any official research or interest in UFOs, and on 27 February, 1968, *Pravda* published an article, signed by three leading science administrators, which declared that people who reported seeing UFOs were either liars, or peasants with no scientific training. The three authors stated that not a single object had been seen over the Soviet Union which could not be explained.

and other witnesses. On 10th November of that year, it was announced that there was to be a full investigation of UFOs. This was announced on Russian television. The operation was to be headed by Major General Anatoly Stolyerov, with Doctor Zigel as Number Two. Thousands of UFO cases were to be analysed by scientists and Soviet Air Force officers. However, the Russian Academy for Sciences came down hard on the new UFO group and on 27th February, 1968, *Pravda* published the official attitude of the authorities, and the cover-up was on.

There is, however, one country which can be relied upon to take a line independent from others over many matters, and UFOs proved to be no exception. In February, 1974, the then French Minister of Defence, M. Robert Galley, was interviewed entirely about UFOs on France-Inter radio station. The interviewer was Jean Claude-Bourret. At the time there was tremendous publicity in France, but for some reason our newspapers did not even mention the broadcast. M. Galley stated that the UFOs were real but admitted that it was not known where they came from. He said that since 1954, there had been a unit in the French Ministry of Defence collecting UFO reports. Some of this material was sent to the National Centre for Space Studies in Toulouse, the French equivalent of the American NASA. In this Centre there was also a unit—a scientific one—studying both UFO sighting and landing reports.

A little over a year ago, I received some information that this particular unit was under government sponsorships and so I put down a Question for Written Answer.

The noble Lord, Lord Donaldson of Kingsbridge, kindly confirmed to me in his reply that the GEPAN unit—those are the initials of the group—had been set up under the French Ministry of Industry, Commerce and Artisans at the centre in Toulouse. M. Galley also added that the gendarmerie were playing a very important part in UFO investigations, questioning witnesses and examining burnt circular marks on the ground where UFOs had landed, or were alleged to have landed. So the French have been taking it all seriously and keeping their own people informed. Nobody panicked and people did not rush like lemmings into the sea.

Is it not time that Her Majesty's Government informed our people of what they know about UFOs? The UFOs have been coming in increasing numbers for 30 years since the war, and I think it is time our people were told the truth. We have not been invaded from outer space. Most incidents have not been hostile. Indeed it is us, the earthlings, who have fired on them. There may have been a few allegedly hostile incidents, but I maintain that if there is a disturbing element in a phenomenon which is pretty friendly on the whole, we should be told the truth. Whatever the truth is, I am sure that an informed public is a prepared one. Another thing: it is on record that both sighting and landing reports are increasing all the time. Just suppose the ufonauts decided to make mass landings tomorrow in this country—there could well be panic here, because our people have not been prepared.

The noble Lord, Lord Strabolgi, is to

reply for Her Majesty's Government at the end of this debate. I should like to ask the noble Lord whether he will contact his right honourable friend the Minister of Defence about the possibility of giving a broadcast interview about UFOs, as his counterpart across the Channel did in 1974. That would go a long way to discredit the view held by a lot of people in this country that there is a cover-up here and that in some way we are playing along with the United States over this. I should also like to see an intra-governmental study of the UFOs. All Governments should get together and pool their knowledge about UFOs, and the results should be passed on to the public. Finally, I should like to thank your Lordships for your kind attention, and I beg to move for Papers.

7.29 p.m.

Lord TREFGARNE: My Lords, I am bound to say that I face making this speech with some trepidation. I had wondered whether we could justify the holding of what is in effect a full debate on this matter; but having seen the audience we have tonight, and indeed having heard the speech of the noble Earl, Lord Clancarty, I can see that that sort of thought would not go down too well. I may well be shouted down before I finish anyway, but let us see if we can avoid that right at the start.

The noble Earl asked us in his Motion to support a proposal particularly for an intra-governmental study—I suppose he means, as indeed he has described, between Governments. No doubt he would wish to see the co-operation of the United States. But I should not want to

LORD TREFARGNE, 37 became Conservative Party Whip in the House of Lords in 1977. After school in England, he went to Princeton University, and then became famous as an aviator, receiving in 1963 a medal from the Royal Aero Club for his flight from England to Australia and back in a light aircraft. He has held several records for flights to Iceland and New York. His other interest is photography. He is married with three children.

support that kind of proposal. I do not think the time has yet come when we can view this matter with sufficient certainty to justify the expenditure of public money on it.

I certainly agree that the numerous voluntary bodies, including those with which the noble Earl is associated, ought to be encouraged, and indeed I should not be opposed to informal links between those bodies—or, at least the responsible ones—and others, such as the Ministry of Defence. But I am ashamed to say, in the midst of all this faith, that I am not myself a believer in UFOs described, as I believe they are, as objects or vehicles from another planet or from another universe.

I have some 2,500 hours as a pilot. I have flown across the atlantic a few times as a pilot. But, unlike with the aircraft reported by the noble Earl, I have never seen one. I presume—indeed, I believe—that a good many of the sightings can be explained by logical

Photograph taken by the pilot of an AVENA Airlines plane between Barcelona and Maiquetia, Venazuela. An interesting feature are the shadows cast by the plane and the object.

Photo right, the late George Adamski, author of several books about the contacts he claimed with UFOs and occupants, beginning with his meeting on 20 November 1952 with the crew of a 'scout ship' from Venus. He developed mediumistic powers and became for a time a favourite of the Queen of the Netherlands.

A wave of UFO sightings was recorded in New Zealand at the beginning of 1979. A series of unknown objects appeared on radar screens and were seen by many witnesses, including airline pilots and members of an Australian television crew, whose film of a round, glowing object was later shown all over the world. Quite as remarkable as the phenomenon itself was the urgent and confused response to it by government scientists and other authorities. Expert after expert proclaimed the whole matter solved and gave authoritative explanations. The objects were variously identified as migrating geese, the lights of fishing boats, meteor showers and a number of different planets – to name but a few. The explanations, being so diverse and inconsistent with each other, the effect was to discredit all official pronouncements on UFOs, and to emphasize to the public that the phenomenon, while ever intensifying, remains as baffling to the authorities as it does to everyone else.

Photographs of the New Zealand phenomenon follow on page 35.

scientific theory and I am, so far at least, convinced that those that cannot so far be so explained could be, if our knowledge were more advanced or if we had more information about the sightings in question. It is these unexplained sightings upon which ufologists rely so heavily in asking us to accept their theories. But I believe, as I say, that these unexplained sightings could be—and, indeed, would be—explained, if we had more knowledge about them; for example, better photographs. How many clear photographs of UFOs have your Lordships seen? All I have seen are hazy, fudgy photographs which could, or could not, be genuine.

Ufologists often rely upon radar information for evidence in their case, but I must tell your Lordships that radar plays more tricks even than the camera, and I do not believe that radar information, in this context, is valid. For example, the recent sightings in New Zealand, which were widely reported just before Christmas, including some rather strange-looking photographs which appeared on television, were also said to have been confirmed by radar information which was available to the aircraft in question. But I know from my own experience that radar is frequently used, and, indeed, is so designed, for detecting anomalies in atmospheric conditions and in weather patterns, and I am not persuaded that radar is a valid supporting argument in this case.

Since time immemorial, man has ascribed those phenomena that he could not explain to some supernatural or extraterrestrial agents. Eventually, as scientific wisdom has advanced, these phenomena are understood more fully, until now, today, no one takes witchcraft seriously

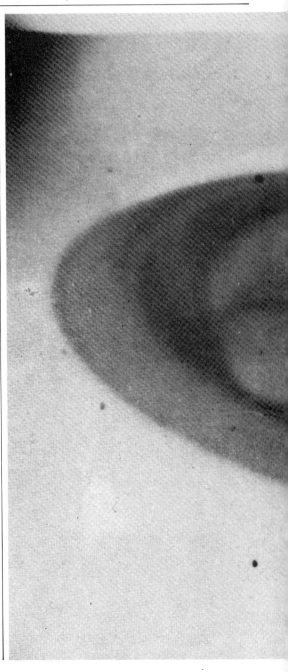

UFO photographs. Most UFO books and magazines contain photographs allegedly taken by witnesses of unknown objects in the sky. The majority, as Lord Trefgarne says, are hazy and could be interpreted in many different ways, from meteorological phenomena to alien space craft. Several notorious fakes continue to go the rounds in UFO publications, while others are genuine, in the sense that they record sightings of unknown aerial phenomena.

The first classic flying saucer photographs, published by George Adamski, in his book with Desmond Leslie, *Flying Saucers Have Landed,* (1953), purported to show the craft in which the beings he encountered on the slopes of Mount Palomar, California, had travelled from Venus. The authenticity of these photographs was challenged in a farcical incident in 1975, when the lid of a bottle cooler in a London restaurant was found to be of exactly the same design as Adamski's Venusian spacecraft. On September 19, the British press headlined exposures of Adamski, assuming that he had photographed bottle cooler lids and passed them off as flying saucers. The amusing sequel was the discovery of the original bottle cooler designer, Mr. Frank Nicholson, who proved that his design of the cooler and lid dated from 1959, six years *after* Adamski published his photographs. Mr. Nicholson was a follower of the UFO mystery and his design

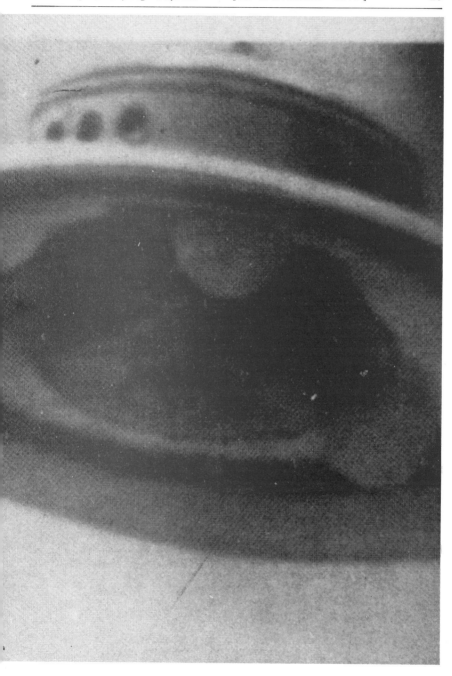

was a tribute to George Adamski! Inevitably the collapse of the anti-Adamski case received far less Press notice than was given to the original slanders

In common with several other UFO photographs which are so detailed that they must be clever fakes of genuine solid flying saucers, Adamski's sharply divide the sceptics from the believers in extra-terrestial spacecraft. Yet several modern UFO writers are beginning to suggest that there may be a third explanation under the general term of projected thought-forms. Adamski was a mystic and a medium, and his powerful imagination certainly helped shape the popular iconography of his generation. There is now considerable evidence of the peculiar ability of certain people to mark the unexposed camera film (see *The World of Ted Serios*, 1968), and sometimes other objects with images formed in the mind (see Michell and Rickard, *Phenomena*, 1977, pages 56-61). The fact that Adamski's images were so reflective of science fiction and cultist ideas of the time, as well as corresponding to archetypal visionary forms (see C.J. Jung, *Flying Saucers: the Modern Myth of Things Seen in the Sky)* suggests the possibility that they may have originated as mental projections.

Illustrations on preceeding pages, the bottle cooler lid which Adamski was falsely accused of photographing as a 'UFO', and one of his flying saucer photographs.

and there are no fairies at the bottom of my garden. It is not so long ago that magnetism, as it occurs naturally in the form of lodestone, was thought to be the work of the Devil, as indeed were some of the hot springs found in Iceland, Australia and elsewhere.

An eclipse of the sun or the moon, now fully understood, was once thought to be an expression of the Almighty's displeasure. Perhaps this derives from the description in the Gospels of the events following the Crucifixion. I recall the 44th and 45th verses of the 23rd chapter of St. Luke's Gospel, and I shall read it if I may:

" And it was about the sixth hour, and there was a darkness over all the earth until the ninth hour.

And the sun was darkened, and the veil of the temple was rent in the midst ".

St. Matthew described it rather well also:

" And, behold, the veil of the temple was rent in twain from the top to the bottom; and the earth did quake, and the rocks rent ".

No one would now seriously doubt that those happenings were, in fact, an eclipse of the sun and an earthquake respectively. I would not deny that there may have been divine intervention in respect of the timing of those events, but certainly I would say that they were caused by terrestrial forces which we now fully understand.

Without wishing to pre-empt anything that the right reverend Prelate the Bishop of Norwich may say, perhaps I may pose the question as to whether the existence of another race or races outside our universe is compatible with our Christian principles. I speak only as a simple member of the Christian faith, but I think I believe that He loves us and us alone. I am not aware that there is any suggestion in the words of Christ or in the words of the Almighty, as recorded that we must share his goodness with people from another universe. There is no suggestion that there is, indeed, any other such people. I acknowledge, however, that, for example, the works of Darwin were once thought incompatible with the Christian faith, and so perhaps my view of the credibility of these things, from a Christian point of view, is open to correction. Perhaps the right reverend Prelate will be able to help us when he comes to speak.

I emphasise that I do not for a moment doubt the sincerity and conviction of those who believe in these objects, who believe that they are visitors from another universe or, at least, some supernatural force beyond our reason. I simply do not happen to agree with them. I certainly do not agree with the learned professor, speaking on the radio the other morning, who said: " Anyone who believes in UFOs is a loony ". But as for the suggestion that an international study group should be set up, I do not think that I could countenance that as a serious proposal at this time. I emphasise, however, that I would be happy to encourage informal links between, for example, the RAF and the very worthy groups who believe differently from the way I do.

Before I sit down, I should just like to say how much I am looking forward to the maiden speech of my noble friend Lord Oxfuird, who is to speak later in the debate. His name has, of course, appeared on the Order Paper before today, and I hope that it appears on the list of speakers a good many times in the future. The noble Earl, Lord Clancarty, has done us a service by bringing this matter forward, but I would counsel caution and care.

7.38 p.m.

LORD KIMBERLEY, a Liberal peer, is a former party spokesman on aviation, aerospace and defense. He is a noted sportsman with an early interest in motor racing, was for many years a member of the British bobsleigh team, and goes in for all field sports, shooting and big game fishing. His interests are now extended to gardening, campaigning against alcohilism, and the study of UFOs. In 1941, Lord Kimberley inherited a great estate in Norfolk, later sold. He has married five times and now lives at Cricklade, Wiltshire.

The Earl of KIMBERLEY: My Lords, as the noble Lord, Lord Trefgarne, has said, the majority of noble Lords in this Chamber will be greatly indebted to the noble Earl, Lord Clancarty, for raising this fascinating and controversial subject this evening. Before I begin, perhaps I should say that I have an interest in it, because I am a director of a company which is to make an identified flying object—a thermo skyship, which is saucer shaped. I shall not get that muddled up. But in spite of sceptics, such as the noble Lord, Lord Wigg, the other day in a newspaper, and Sir Bernard Lovell from Jodrell Bank, who says that UFOs do not exist, we must agree that they do, because otherwise there would be no unidentified flying objects. Furthermore, we should not have throughout the world radio telescopes listening to try to pick up signals from intelligences in outer space.

As the noble Earl, Lord Clancarty, said, UFOs are not products of the 20th century imagination. They have been observed here for years—by the North American Indians, by the monks of Byland Abbey in 1290, who were terrified by the appearance of a huge silver disc. Right through history up to today, millions of people have seen UFOs, and I will go so far as to say that I am the first to admit that the very large majority

The Byland Abbey sighting in January 1290 was first introduced into UFO literature by Desmond Leslie, quoting from a manuscript discovered in 1953 at Ampleforth in Yorkshire.

"Took the sheep from Wilfred and roasted them on the feast

of them can be explained as natural or man-made phenomena—meteorites, satellite débris, weather balloons, military flares, *et cetera*. But there are still many which are completely unexplained.

It has been reported that the United States and the USSR signed a pact in 1971 to swop UFO information, but the pact stated that they were to keep the rest of the world in the dark. I believe that the pact was signed so that neither super-Power would make mistakes about UFOs being atomic missiles. I am also led to understand that quite recently the three United States balloonists who crossed the Atlantic were followed for up to 12 hours by UFOs but were ordered by United States Government agents not to discuss them.

We know that war in space, once a figment of the imagination and a subject much beloved by science fiction writers, is very nearly a fact now. Both super-Powers have, or will have, killer satellites and laser beams operating in space. May I ask the noble Lord, Lord Strabolgi, whether he agrees that this may perhaps be one of the reasons for the reticence of the United States over being more forthcoming about their UFO information?

In 1977, Sir Eric Gairy, the Prime Minister of Grenada, backed by President Carter, wanted the United Nations to declare 1978 as the Year of the UFO. They both failed. However, the proposition was finally tabled for 29th September 1978. This proposition was postponed through October, November and December. It was finally threatened by the veto of the United States and Russia. Hopefully, however, it will now be considered

of SS. Simon and Jude. But when Henry the abbot was about to say grace, John, one of the brethren, came in and said there was a great portent outside. Then they all ran out and Lo! a large round silver thing like a disc (res grandia, circum-circularis argentae, disco quondam haud dissimilis) flew slowly over them and excited the greatest terror."

Prime Minister Gairy with some of the international team of UFO investigators whom he assembled to advise him in presenting his case before the United Nations for a UN study of UFOs. Shown here *(left to right)* are Len Stringfield, UFO writer; Sir Eric Gairy; Dr. Gordon Cooper, astronaut; Lee Spiegel, UFO consultant; Dr. J. Allen Hynek, veteran UFO investigator and author.

On 28 November 1977 the Special Political Committee of the United Nations General Assembly held the first UN debate on UFOs. The resolution, put by Sir Eric Gairy, Prime Minister of Grenada in the West Indies, called for the setting up of a special UN department to conduct and co-ordinate research into UFOs, and for 1978 to be declared International Year of Unidentified Flying Objects.

Sir Eric Gairy opened the debate by describing a UFO sighting of his own 2½ years earlier.

in June of this year. I believe that at last there has been a unanimous vote that the proposition will not be rejected.

As the noble Lord, Lord Trefgarne, said, I agree entirely that we do not understand many of these unidentified flying objects because of our lack of knowledge. UFOs defy worldly logic. Even if one accepts that there may be life elsewhere in our galaxy, or even in other galaxies, the human mind cannot begin to comprehend UFO characteristics: their propulsion, their sudden appearance, their disappearance, their great speeds, their silence, their manoeuvres, their apparent anti-gravity, their changing shapes. They defy our present knowledge and laws of matter. Of course, this naturally upsets our earthly scientists because it is outside their earthly terms of reference and knowledge, but to try to present UFOs in a more mundane light let us briefly examine the last 30 years.

In 1947, the United States Air Force started an official project called " SIGN ". By 1949, 243 reports of UFOs had been submitted, but no conclusive evidence came to the public's knowledge from this project. Project Blue Book was then born, and its findings produced the same conclusions. So it appears that the United States Air Force concern was threefold: first, to see whether UFOs were a threat to the security of the United States; secondly, to see whether UFOs could contribute technical and scientific knowledge; and, thirdly, to explain to the general American public what was going on in their air space. However, as UFOs appeared to offer no threat to security, Project Blue Book became just a public relations exercise to not inform the public, despite numerous unidentified radar trackings and close approaches made by UFOs to both civil and military aircraft. The military staff in America said that, as there was no threat or danger, they were not interested in pursuing the subject any further. So Project Blue Book was abandoned.

This may be good enough to fob off the American public, but it is not good enough to fob off the British public. Too many people—ordinary people as well as famous people—have seen UFOs. Ten Governments now openly admit that UFOs exist and are real: France, Norway, Sweden, Brazil, the Argentine, Venezuela, Mexico, the Philippines, Peru and Grenada. Other Governments know that UFOs exist but do not admit it publicly. President

"I saw a UFO as I was driving home at about two or three in the morning. It was a big object, a brilliant light, golden bright, moving at tremendous speed."

He went on to say that he had been encouraged to instigate the debate by news that President Carter had also seen a UFO.

The Grenada UN delegate, Mr. Wellington Friday, continued the debate with a speech lasting an hour and a half in which he referred to a number of 'contactee' and UFO abduction cases, and pleaded that "the amorphous veil of secrecy" surrounding these reports be lifted by means of a full United Nations investigation.

Some three quarters of the 149 United Nations member states sent delegates to the meeting. Grenada officials entertained them with a showing of *Close Encounters of the Third Kind*, and distributed UFO books and copies of Sir Eric's and Mr. Friday's speeches.

On 12 March, 1979, while he was in New York arranging for the renewed UFO debate to be held later that year, Sir Eric Gairy was removed from office in a coup by rival Grenada politicians. Unable to return home, he continues privately as a UFO evangelist in the United States.

Project Sign, renamed the following year Project Grudge, and later Project Blue Book, was the agency set up by the US Air Force to monitor and assess UFO reports in relation to national security. Its date of foundation was 22nd. January 1948, two weeks after an event which shocked Air Force officials- the death of pilot Thomas Mantell when his plane crash- ed during pursuit of an un- known object described as "metallic and tremendous in size" near Louisville, Kentucky

From the start, the Project's directors were criticised for their policy in public state- ments of explaining away, while ignoring inexplicable aspects in UFO cases sub- mitted to them. In August 1948, staff members pro- duced a report entitled 'Estimate of the Situation' which concluded that UFOs were most likely inter- planetary spacecraft. This report was suppressed by General Vandenberg, the Air Force Chief of Staff, and was never released. In disappointment, several of its more active members re- signed from the Project, and little was heard of it until, on December 27 the follow- ing year, its publication of the 'Grudge Report' re- kindled public and official interest in the UFO pheno- menon. It revealed that of the 237 UFO cases studied by the Project, 23% could not be explained in terms of possible known causes. The scientist mainly responsible for this analysis was Dr. J. Allen Hynek, consultant astro- nomer to the Project; and in October 1968 Dr. Hynek addressed a letter to the Director of the project, denouncing it as biased and unscientific in its approach and worthless to serious students of the UFO problem. He referred to Blue Book as "the Society for the Ex- planation of the Uninvesti- gated."

Carter has personally seen a UFO.

Let me give a small sample of promi- nent, scientific and sane people who have seen UFOs or believe, through evidence, that they exist: Commander Robert McLaughlin, United States Navy missile expert; John McCormack, Speaker, United States House of Representatives; the late Air Chief Marshall Lord Dowding; the late President Truman; Dr. Stanton Friedman, United States Nuclear Physi- cist; Ed Mitchell, Apollo astronaut; Gordon Cooper, Apollo astronaut; Dr. Allen Hynek, Professor of Astronomy, North West University; Walter Cronkite, United States newscaster; Neil Armstrong, first man on the moon; and, lastly, Dr. Felix Zigel, Professor of Higher Mathe- matics and Astronomy, Moscow Aero- nautical Institute. Can any of your Lordships sincerely believe that these aforementioned people all suffer either from hallucinations or believe in fairy stories?

Despite the United States and the USSR embargo on UFO information, funnily enough the Russians appear more inclined to think that UFOs have extra-terrestrial origins. Further, some Russian scientists see a connection between UFOs and paranormal phenomena. In fact, there is an ever-growing belief that space travel has a connection with tele- pathy and telekinesis, because cosmonauts in orbit have discovered through scientific tests that they have an increased level of telephathic communication. If we assume that extra-terrestrial intelligences who travel to earth are more advanced than we are—and in that respect I think that they must be—then UFOs could be tele- kinetic phenomena: in other words, controlled by thought pulses.

Since thought is not subject to the physical limitations of matter, then velocities in excess of the speed of light would be possible. It is interesting to me that in 1968 I was speaking to Sir Frank Whittle, the inventor of the jet engine and an eminent scientist, about interstellar space travel. It was just before the Americans had landed on the moon. Sir Frank said that he thought that it would be perfectly feasible one day to go to the stars, as he did not believe in Einstein's theory of relativity. A remark like this, coming from an ordinary man like myself, would probably, quite rightly, be laughed at. But one can certainly not laugh when a remark like that is made by such an eminent person as Sir Frank Whittle.

What is interesting is that two years later, in 1970, Dr. Fomin, a Russian doctor of telekinesis and automation, argued that, to traverse interstellar space, we would have to grapple with physical laws different from those we know at present and which so far are only theory. However, these principles have been established in mathematical formulae. Therefore, Einstein's concept of time and space possibly may not apply.

In 1976, President Carter, in a pre-election pledge stated:

" If I become President, I'll make every piece of information this country has about UFO sitings available to the public and the scientists. I am convinced that UFOs exist. I have seen them ".

This statement was a breakthrough against the United States cover-up as it admitted that not all UFO information is, or has been, available to the American public. For instance, do your Lordships' know

Project Blue Book, which received its name in April 1952, was officially terminated on 17 December 1969, and its work is now carried on in secret bys an agency of the Aerospace Defence Command.

There has long been debate about the extent to which government and defence institutions cover up evidence of UFO activity. The UFO literature is full of cases where photographs and documents relating to UFOs have disappeared after being submitted for analysis to official bodies, whether through carelessness, in the interests of security or from other causes. It is also alleged that owners of such evidence are often robbed of it or forced to part with it in face of threats by mysterious visitors. See e.g. Gordon Creighton's *'On Disappearing UFO Photographs,' Flying Saucer Review, March/April 1970.* Some of these incidents may simply reflect the nervous excitement of UFO witnesses; others are less easily explained.

Several UFO writers, including Hynek and Vallee, have claimed first hand knowledge of UFO evidence officially suppressed, specifically during progress of sky photography at satellite-tracking stations. If they are right, the evidence still exists, but no one has yet cared for the task of searching it out from among the many square miles of sky film preserved in the vaults of the Smithsonian Astrophysical Laboratory.

that three former United States Presidents before their election proclaimed their belief in UFOs? They were President Eisenhower, President Lyndon Johnson and President Ford, who I agree was appointed. During their presidencies they became completely silent and did not fulfil their promises. Why? I strongly suspect that Her Majesty's Government know why, and if they do know, why then, they should inform your Lordships.

I believe that there is much material evidence on UFOs in the national archives in the United States of America which has never been made known to the public, and even President Carter is finding it difficult to carry out his pre-election pledge. I am led to believe that he has tried unsuccessfully with NASA to do UFO research. The answer he has been given is " No, due to expense ". That research which NASA has been required to do would cost a few million dollars, but a few million dollars is only the cost of two astronauts' suits. Therefore it appears obvious that for some reason there is a cover-up in the United States.

We in the United Kingdom are in a strange position because we have had thousands of sightings, yet I am led to understand that the Ministry of Defence have only two clerks working on UFO sightings. Further, they claim that they are not spending any money on UFO research. They appear reluctant to investigate publicly connected phenomena such as alleged messages from outer space. They say that this is the responsibility of the BBC and the Post Office. Can the Minister say whether the BBC and the Post Office know that they have this responsibility?

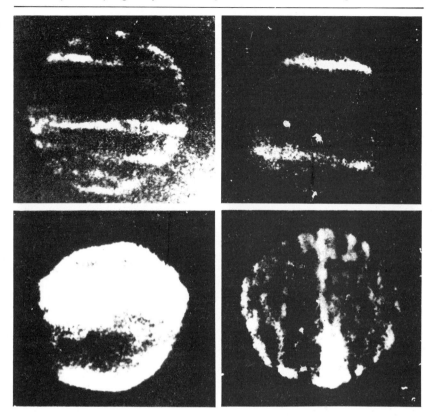

Further, when the noble Lord, Lord Strabolgi, replies to the debate will he confirm that Her Majesty's Government might be sympathetic and give support to the efforts of President Carter, Dr. Kurt Waldheim and Sir Eric Gairy to get the United Nations to debate the resolution

"to discover the origin, nature and intent of UFOs".

The noble Earl, Lord Clancarty, said that we should set up a parliamentary UFO group to meet a few times a year. I would concur with him. Further, I think the general public should be encouraged to come forward with evidence. Many do not, for fear of being ridiculed.

Views of the object filmed by a television crew from an aeroplane over New Zealand on 31 December, 1978.

```
CONTACTS FOR THE YEAR ENDED 22/2/78 (23) AS FOLLOWS:
K5634    J.MITCHELL        LEICESTER     559/7C      CLASS  5    23/ 5/77 6935
K5635    O.KRAMER          BRADFORD      11A/?       CLASS  5    24/ 5/77 1116
K5636    D.M.SMITH         LONDON (SW)   559/7C      CLASS  3    16/ 6/77 0600
K5637    F.W.SHOEMAKER
K5638    K.L.DOORS         LONDON (SW)   559/7C      CLASS  5    23/ 7/77 1755
K5639    T.BETTS           FALMOUTH      558/0'X     CLASS  2D   23/ 7/77 1721
K5640    W.M.GRANGER       LLANELLI      555/C4S     CLASS  5     1/ 8/77 0931
K5641 S.D.D.PATEL          SOUTHALL      640 OKW/2   CLASS 16    11/ 9/77 1159
K5642 S.L.D.O'BRIEN        LEEDS         559/7C      CLASS  5    18/10/77 0445
K5643    T.MCNAMARA        BELFAST       038/23      CLASS 16    22/11/77 2350
K5644    B.F.WEST          ABERDEEN      088/23      CLASS  6    23/11/77 0020
K5645    T.BRANDENBURGER   SLOUGH        559/7C      CLASS  5    14/12/77 1807
K5646    F.K.SKINNER       BELPER        H6/44/46    CLASS 16    23/12/77 2300
K5647    W.W.WRIGHT        DERBY         559/KW      CLASS  5    31/12/77 1305
K5648    T.M.SLABY         TRURO         559/?       CLASS  8     2/ 1/78 0430
K5649    D.W.MARCUS        SELBY         1080/46     CLASS 16    23/ 1/78 1056
K5650    A.ANDREWS         GLASGOW       559SERIES   CLASS  5     1/ 2/78 0945
K5651    D.T.SMEDLEY       LONDON (E)    7A/7C       CLASS 23    22/ 2/78 1201
```

The mysterious list of UFO contacts, referred to by Lord Kimberley, is the classified document *UFO/45/MEMO/666/78*, sent to the following organizations: Metropolitan Police; Defence (Air Force); Defence (Civil); Special Patrol Groups; BBC (Intelligence Branch); Sub-Regional Controls; Computer Data Section; Microwave Communications Network

The enigmatic list as published in the magazine *Viewpoint Aquarius*, July, 1978, reads as above.

Let them be open; let them be honest; let them badger their Member of Parliament and the Government to be open with them and to cease what I am convinced is a cover-up here. The people of Britain have a right to know all that the Governments, not only of this country but others throughout the world, know about UFOs.

Before I sit down I ask the noble Lord, Lord Strabolgi, whether he will tell your Lordships why the Ministry of Defence has not informed the public of 18 contacts from 23rd May 1977 up to 22nd February 1978, numbered K 5634 to K 5651 inclusive. Further, what do the classification numbers 5, 3, 20, 16, 6, 8 and 23 mean for these 18 contacts? Moreover, does the noble Lord realise that 13 out of these 18 contacts were seen during the hours of daylight? There need be no fear that the people of this country may panic, since if UFOs are extra-terrestrial their intelligence and knowledge is far ahead of our primitive understanding. My Lords, I heartily support the Motion moved by the noble Earl, Lord Clancarty, for an intra-governmental body to research UFOs. Let Her Majesty's Government give an example to the rest of the world by being the leader in this investigation.

7.55 p.m.

The Viscount of OXFUIRD: My Lords, first I should like to thank the noble Earl, Lord Clancerty, for initiating this extremely interesting debate. Of course it is really much above my head, but I have enjoyed it already and I hope I shall enjoy it for the rest of the evening. To me, the first question really is, where have these UFOs come from? There could be a great many answers to that, but in the first place we can look at our own planet and there is no doubt that there is very little chance of their having come from anything in our own solar system. In fact I think I should quote a few words from Professor Kopal's recent book on the solar system which finishes up, after lamenting the fact of what they found out about Mars, by saying:

" The hope of finding life on Mars has evaporated, together with the canals, into the thin Martian air. It is now almost certain that as living beings we are alone in the solar system ".

I think that is a very good example of the fact that we cannot look to the solar system to discover where these things come from, if they come from anywhere.

The next possibility which has been paraded is that they might come from the sister sun in our own galaxy. Of course that is quite possible if you believe in the now accepted—or shall we say more popular—theory of the " big bang " for the start of the universe. Undoubtedly, our sun and its solar system must have

LORD OXFUIRD, formerly Sir Donald Makgill, became a Viscount in 1977, when the House of Lords Committee for Privileges allowed his claim to an ancient and dormant title. He is aged 79, lives in Scotland with his second wife and spends much of his time fishing.

The praise given to his speech by later contributors to the debate arises from the conventional politeness of the House of Lord's to a peer's maiden speech and from the general desire to congratulate Lord Oxfuird on finally establishing his lawful rights.

Robert Temple, who was present at the debate and reported it for the UFO magazine, *Second Look*, described Lord Oxfuird as "a dignified, slender, white-haired man, holding a sort of electronic ear trumpet to one ear...He had the quaint habit of turning on his seat to face each speaker in turn, and, as he was offered congratulations, Oxfuird would stiffly and properly bow from the waist, his face lit with a happy and dignified smile, and his ear trumpet clutched to his ear accompanying each bow."

been shared with many others at that moment when we suddenly appeared. They even give dates for it now; they talk about 5,000 million years ago, which fits in with our own geological background.

There are many stars which have a solar system which might well be in the same position; they might have one planet, as we have, as good as ours and with the same amount of knowledge. On the other hand, we must accept the fact, as the noble Earl, Lord Kimberley, was saying, that it would have to be something which we have not been able to attain on this earth and something that we do not understand on this earth, because if one wanted to get, say, from A Centauri, which is our nearest star, to here, it would take half a lifetime. Even travelling faster than anything we have ever produced in the way of space ships in this world of ours, the distance is 250,000 times the distance that we are from our sun, which is 93 million miles. It is a distance which would certainly take half a lifetime, even at 100,000 miles an hour. So I do not think it would be reasonable to look at another solar system, say A Centauri, which is very near, being only roughly $4\frac{1}{4}$ light years from us, which is not very much in space. There is of course the possibility that the UFOs may come from some secret effort on this earth. This I very much doubt because one could not keep a thing like that secret for 20 or 30 years. I very much doubt the possibility of its being on this earth.

So we get an entirely different picture. We have progressed in the last 30 years both in cosmology and in many other sciences, more than we have ever done

before, certainly in my lifetime. I think
the feeling really is that we are now on the
edge of something in the universe which
we do not understand yet. However, if
we are going to understand the UFO
question, we have got to move to the
extent of understanding something beyond
cosmology today. From our point of
view, what we are looking at is the tip
of the iceberg. We know perfectly well
that we get information, we put it into
computers and come out at the other
end with a new model. Then in five or
10 years the model is thrown away and
we are back with the one answer which
applies, unfortunately, to so much of
science today; we just do not know.
But one hopes that it will be possible.

If the suggestion of the noble Earl,
Lord Clancarty, backed by the noble
Earl, Lord Kimberley, is adopted—that is,
that we should have a worldwide organisation—to look into this matter and to go
further than we have ever done, why
should we not be the leaders of it? It
would twist science back into a new
field. Is it possible that there is not
merely another solar system in our galaxy,
but that somewhere in one of the many
galaxies in the expanding universe there
are other places where these things could
come from with their amazingly vast
scientific knowledge? I personally see
no valid reason why we must accept that
at this time, but we should start working
for it. If we had a worldwide organisation to try to control that, perhaps we
should be able to solve many of the
problems which face us today in the
universe; and nothing could be better.
Then we might possibly find the answer
to our UFOs.

LORD DAVIES OF LEEK, 74, was Labour M.P. for Leek in Staffordshire for 25 years from 1945 and held government office in the 1960's. In 1965 he was sent by the Prime Minister as a special envoy on a peace mission to Hanoi. He was trained and worked as a schoolmaster, and has written extensively in the press on educational, social and Far Eastern matters. His chief interests are sport and politics, and he was made a life peer in 1970.

8.2 p.m.

Lord DAVIES of LEEK: My Lords, as the lone figure on this side of the House who has dared to come in on this debate, may I say that it has been a pleasure to listen to the noble Viscount, Lord Oxfuird, who has just spoken and, who has, in his own inimitable way, as a result of his military and other experience over the years, brought a certain depth and profundity to the request for some investigation into the phenomenon with which mankind is presented today. Consequently, with all sincerity I can say that I hope this House will have the pleasure of listening to the noble Viscount on many occasions adding his voice to our deliberations, and I thank him for what he has said.

Now I want to attack the problem in my own way. First, I want to ask what are we talking about. Secondly, after expressing my gratitude for the maiden Speech, I would also express thanks to the noble Earl, Lord Clancarty, who initiated this debate to call attention to the increasing number of sightings and landings on a worldwide scale of un-identified flying objects. There is no argument about that. Do not let the noble Earl be a little bit sad because of dandy intellectualism that may approach this debate. The world oozes with intellectuality and at the present moment it is completely lacking in wisdom. Let us remember what I have said many times here, and it was my old mother who taught me this; she made me go to Sunday school and quote the text. She would say in Welsh: " Always remember, my boy, Solomon did not ask for cleverness, he asked for wisdom ". There is a vast difference between the dandy intellectualism of some of the reporters on newspapers' approach to this problem and the wise approach that we have just heard in this maiden speech. Let us anchor that down. What else does the noble Earl ask for. He says on a worldwide scale and that there is need for intergovernmental study. I will add to it from the other side of the House that the expense would be so small that we should not neglect this.

Anybody who knows something about laser beams—and I saw in a laboratory in Switzerland for the first time the effect of a laser beam—knows it would be quite possible to throw on to that table now an identified or unidentified object that would look palpable, like Macbeth's dagger. Your Lordships remember the famous dagger scene:

" Is this a dagger I see before me
The handle toward my hand? . . .
In form as palpable
As this which now I draw ".

We could with a laser beam throw a dagger that would look as palpable on to that table. There may be an understanding of the power of the laser and its effect existing in some kind of technology that is beyond the dimension in which we can work. We have been looking in mathematics for the fifth and even the sixth dimension.

I had better pick up my notes, lest we be here a long time. Noble Lords need not worry; so much has been quoted that it saves me a lot of quotation. I want to ask the 64,000 dollar question. Do noble Lords believe in angels? The answer from some will be, Yes, and yet they have never seen one. We are asking you to believe in the phenomena of flying saucers, seen by now by, I should think, probably millions, at any rate hundreds of thousands, without exaggeration. If we are studying hagiography—and I had better be careful—which is the history of the saints, if I came off my Welsh mountains and came down as a little boy of 12 and said I had seen the Virgin Mary springing out of a rock, some devout religious people would believe me; but if I said I had seen a flying saucer they would not believe me. What is the difference? It is a question that has to be asked; it is a philosophical question that has to be asked, when intellectuality, in its pompous way in its Sunday newspaper articles, is dealing in print with mysteries that Shakespeare described—to misquote him: " There is more in heaven and earth than is thought of in man's philosophy ".

So this deserves not being pushed aside. Mark you, my Lords, I was told today outside those doors that an ambassador of 8 ft. 6 ins. with green feet and webbed feet as well had asked whether he could park his flying saucer in our car park, according to some of the telephones that have been ringing here today, because some people have treated the whole matter as a joke. I would, therefore, suggest to them that they read H. G. Wells' *Final Essay*. They can read it in half an hour. It is slim, it is cogent, it is succinct. He says the human mind is **at** the end of its tether.

There is a queerness in the cosmology of the world in which we are now living. Was Wells right? We certainly see mankind acting queer when petrol is short.

He is snarling and worse than any being from outer space. The anthropological arrogance of 20th century man in his tinpot motor-cars riding through the streets of the lovely spaceship we call the world is hartbreaking. He has learnt nothing from his two wars; and if we had another, God help mankind, in view of the way that he has shown his greed, selfishness and tendency to panic as never before since the days of the Crusades. The greatest delusion in the history of man was the delusion of the Crusades. But men went on them after the days of Peter the Hermit with a fiery and fierce belief in what they were doing.

The noble Earl, Lord Clancarty, is an expert who has been written about. In fact, he dropped everything else to write about this matter. His seven books have been translated into many languages and I congratulate him. He has done a job of work and I hope that the debate initiated by the noble Earl will receive some attention. People tend to scoff, but it is only a few days ago that we were sitting at the piano, playing and knocking out—nct with the brilliance of a top pianist—" We three kings of Orient are ". What did they follow? They followed a star. What was that star? We have had an intellectual analysis of why after the Crucifixion darkness spread over the earth. The noble Lord, Lord Trefgarne— who has piloted from one side of the ocean to the other—made intellectual assumptions about earthquakes and eclipses. We are not completely sure how to explain eclipses or earthquakes, but we have a kind of Kepler mathematics that times things rather nicely. It is not quite enough to explain the earthquakes. It

The incident as Pascagoula took place on 11 October 1973. It is impressive as being one of the best documented and most critically investigated of all 'UFO contactee' cases. Two local shipyard workers, Charles Hickson, 42, and Calvin Parker, 19, went to the police in a state of terror and near-collapse with the story that they had been taken on board a UFO and examined by strange creatures.
At about 7 p.m. they were fishing in the Pascagoula River when they noticed a blue light in the sky. The light descended and an unknown craft, about 8 feet high and "sort of oblong" hovered two or three feet above the river near the two men. One end of the craft opened and three weird creatures, like robots (see drawing), floated out of it and levitated the men inside. Their experience within the craft was of weightless suspension in a glowing chamber, while an instrument like a great eye scanned their bodies. About half an hour later they found themselves back on the river bank and saw the craft take off and vanish.
Interrogation of the two men throughout the night by police, doctors, psychiatrists and security agents left no investigator in doubt that they had undergone a genuine, traumatic experience and were sincere in their accounts of it. Tests with lie-detectors and under hypnosis failed to bring out inconsistencies in or between their stories. For an account of first-hand investigation of the case, see Ralph and Judy Blum's *Beyond Earth* (1974).

does not mean that the mystery of the UFOs is something that can be brushed aside, and it is an anthropological arrogance to so say.

Good heavens, I have been speaking for nine minutes! My Lords, do not worry, I shall be about another five. The House has heard a number of laudable people quoted. Ordinary little people have sometimes been laughed at, especially those concerned in the famous sighting at Pascagoula in Mississippi when one little fellow fainted when he saw a chap with one leg jumping towards him with a wizened and wrinkled face, with pointed ears, crab claws for hands, slits for eyes and holes beneath his nostrils—they would not be nostrils without holes, at least I should hope so! We shall not develop fantastic descriptions like that. We shall not go into those realms. But we must say that there are many people who have said that they have experienced these phenomena.

I agree that the New Zealand incident has reawakened man's interest and as the noble Lord, Lord Trefgarne, said, they were not clear pictures. However, I attended a scientific lecture in this noble building not so long ago, given by someone who believed faithfully in the Loch Ness monster. He showed us masses of films. He was a scientist and he swore that the Loch Ness monster existed. There is just as much case for the existence of flying saucers. We know that they exist. All we are saying is that they are unidentified. They may be terrestrial or celestial. We are asking Governments to find an answer and that is all that this debate is about. There is no magic, we have nothing up our sleeves, but let the world know what is going on.

This renewed interest poses many problems and there are many research organisations which are looking into the matter and which know that they exist, but I shall not bore the House by going into them now. Let us ask a couple of questions. How can a flying saucer fly faster than sound and not create a supersonic boom? What is it? Secondly, have we the right to assume that we alone are in the universe? This anthropomorphic view of God that some people have built up does not build for the spirit and does not, I think, build for true holiness. It does not build up for real Christian spirit if it is followed too fully. Therefore, I should say that we have no right to assume that we are the only intelligent beings in the universe. Is the earth the only planet populated by intelligent technological life? I do not know and I do not suppose that we shall be able to find an answer yet. If in a year of Queen Elizabeth I had said to someone in London that I could show him a picture of Philip of Spain in Madrid on a piece of glass in his room, I would probably have been burnt at the stake as a wizard, or as a witch if I were a woman. However, we can do that today. We have broken through. We have the miracle on earth of television, even from the moon.

Are there flying saucers? Can these objects be explained? There are two basic facts. First, the scientific examination of the probability. That is due to mankind and Governments should look into it. The second aspect is to fathom the possibilities of the existence of this phenomena. Astronomers are now increasing their search for extra-territorial radio signals, but so far—despite what the noble Earl, Lord Kimberley, has said—none has really or truly been discovered. The billions of stars in the galaxy make the problem at present too much for us.

Then there is the question of speed. In a light year a ray of light travels 6 trillion miles, but we do not want to go into that. The question of relativity is interesting. I am not qualified to argue about it: I never reached that standard of mathematics. However, I know that Einstein believed that electro magnetic waves have no mass and are therefore not affected by his theory. However, he said that as an object—if it has mass—approaches the speed of light, its mass becomes infinite. That might explain the black holes about which we talk. We are talking of mysteries that we never knew anything about.

For a couple of generations now thousands of magazines and so on have reported these sightings. We want to know whether these objects that are unidentified deserve real research in depth. Whether or not it is true, only our prejudices can decide, and it becomes more difficult to listen to such weird experiences from apparently honest, sane and unself-seeking men who place their findings before papers and Governments. Are we right to call these men liars, hallucinators or sensationalists? If one human being out of the tens of thousands who allege to have seen these phenomena is telling the truth, then there is a dire need for us to look into the matter. Those who believe in psychic phenomena or spiritualism and those who believe in the synchronicity of ghosts—as they try to explain them—should not scoff at the possibility of these unidentified objects. We know that poltergeists exist; we know about their activities. Therefore, do not be so ready to scoff at UFOs when, in another moment if I catch you talking, you will agree with me that poltergeists exist. This is a serious Debate. It deserves study and understanding.

THE BISHOP OF NORWICH is the Rt. Rev. Maurice Arthur Ponsonby Wood, 62. During the war he was a naval chaplain, and he is still Chaplain to the Commando Association. He has written five books on the comforts of Christianity, including *Like A Mighty Army* and *Your Suffering.* His interests, apart from Liturgical Reform, include hockey, tennis, swimming, painting and watching Norwich City play football. He has two sons and one daughter by his first wife, who died in 1954. He remarried the following year and has another two boys and one girl by his second wife.

8.30 p.m.

The Lord Bishop of NORWICH: My Lords, I count it a privilege to follow the noble Viscount, Lord Oxfuird, and to link myself with the words of the noble Lord, Lord Davies of Leek, in congratulating the noble Viscount on his maiden speech. At the beginning of his speech I jotted down that I should like to thank him for his " down-to-earth remarks ", but when he got right out to A Centauri I realised that that phrase was of no use anyway. However, we congratulate him and look forward to hearing his voice again and often.

I am glad to be able to follow—without of course the Welsh fire or fervour—what the noble Lord, Lord Davies of Leek said. I have a little Irish blood in my veins and that is why I understand everything he says. I am sure that the request by the noble Earl, Lord Clancarty:

" To call attention to the increasing number of sightings and landings on a world-wide scale of unidentified flying objects "

is a proper one. I am most glad that we have brought this whole issue out into the open and have been given the unhurried opportunity of talking about it tonight.

It is right that we should give a cool and scientific look at all unidentified flying objects, not only because of natural curiosity, not even only—as I think the noble Earl, Lord Kimberley, suggested— because of national security but also for reasons of scientific research. There was a time when leaders in the Church were not always so enthusiastic about pushing out the frontiers of knowledge as I believe we are today. I very much hope that such a search will continue. Whether or not it should be an intra-governmental study I

am not sure. We shall listen with interest
to what the noble Lord, Lord Strabolgi,
says to us on that. But that it should be
studied, and seriously studied, I believe
to be true.

The interesting thing is that when a
suggested UFO is seen in one part of the
world it seems to spark off many sightings
in other parts. The fact of the New
Zealand sightings a short time ago seems
to have produced many sightings in
Norfolk; and our *Eastern Daily Press*—
which is a magnificent daily paper, accurate
fair and always helpful to the Church—
has told us all about this recently. When
I was talking on television at lunchtime
today in Norwich my immediate reaction
was to ring up the commanding officer of
one of our stations—and for the sake of
national security I shall not name the
actual establishment lest other ears in other
spaces should be listening to me—to ask
whether (and I am quite serious about
this), when sightings were suggested in
Norfolk last week, one of our particularly
important RAF stations had anything to
say about them.

I think that we should be quite cool,
firm and scientific and try to extend our
knowledge in this area. But, with the
wealth of scientific, aeronautical and
erudite knowledge in your Lordships'
House, what is a bishop doing moving
among the various parts of this chequered
chessboard? I felt that I wanted to share
anxieties on a rather narrow level with your
Lordships. First, I believe that UFOs
and the mystery surrounding them today
are helping to build up a climate of
credulity and, in certain cases, even of
superstition, with the danger of a sort of

ersatz spirituality almost reacting against the impersonality of modern civilisation, but not wholly involved in the total Christian commitment, which is a balanced commitment. Last summer at our Lambeth Conference the phrase was used:

" The Church gathers for worship; the Church scatters for mission ".

Those are the two sides of activity: the Church of God meets to worship God but the Church of Christ scatters to spread the good news of the Gospel. My concern here is that the mystery surrounding UFOs today—and I think it is helped by the variety of films and programmes on the subject—is in danger of producing a 20th century superstition in our modern and scientific days which is not unlike the superstition of past years. That is my first anxiety.

The second is that UFOs and their study seem, from my limited research in this area, to link with a certain religious subculture which seems to do three things. It offers a substitute for true, catholic religion. I use " catholic " with a small ' c '; I mean the Christian faith in its widest, but received, sense. Secondly, I think it draws serious, sincere and often very charming people—and young people too—into a sub-Christian, and I am afraid sometimes a non-Christian cult, often controlled by a dominant leader, and reproduces something of the gnostic —I suppose one wants to help people by saying " g-nostic "—heresies of the tight-knit, esoteric groups of the first, second and third centuries. In fact, I believe that Archbishop William Temple was right when he said the Church of Christ was the only society founded for its non-members to take what it knew of God and of Christ into the world that others might know too.

I see a certain danger of the linking of religion with the UFO situation at that level. Some Christian researchers suggest that those who become deeply involved in the religious aspects of the UFO situation come under a psychic domination which can cause serious distress to them and to their personal life. That is my anxiety. I may be wrong, but I put it forward with some care, having thought about it and studied it a good deal. Therefore, my third anxiety—and I am sorry to be negative but it is important to share both the light and the dark sides —is the danger of the religious aspect of the UFO situation leading to the obscuring of basic Christian truths. When all is said and done, Christ himself is the agent of God in the creation of the world. I quote from *Colossians*:

" Christ is the image of the invisible God, the first-born of all creation: for in Christ all things were created in heaven and on earth, visible and invisible—whether thrones or dominions, or principalities or authorities . . . All things were created through Him and for Him ".

This fascinating chapter in *Colossians*, which is perhaps one of the highest levels of Christological teaching, speaks of Christ being before all things: " by him all things consist ", as the Authorised Version put it. All things hold together; He is the great unifying, holding-together principle of God's universe.

I say this in this debate recognising the danger of, as it were, preaching a sermon. However, I do not think that is true in this case because the very subject we are debating is helping to widen our horizons

The question of the theological status of extraterrestrial and other beings not of our race has long exercised subtle minds. Fairies and such-like creatures do not, according to the Church, share with Christians the blessings of Redemption, but the ecclesiastical position on inhabitants of other planets is less cut-and-dried due to the impossibility so far of ascertaining, first, whether they exist, and secondly, whether the Son of God has been incarnate among them. St. Augustine in *City of God,* argued that there were beings in Heaven living in a state of grace, and this view was supported by a papal statement from Pius X11, who supposed that men living in other worlds might never have experienced the Fall and expulsion from Eden, and would therefore not have needed a divine visitation to redeem them.

All who ponder such matters will be gratified to see the old question given another airing in this debate.

—and the noble Viscount, Lord Oxfuird, stressed this point of looking far out in his maiden speech. I believe that Christ has not only a terrestial, not only a cosmic significance but literally a galactic significance. I believe that He is God's vice-regent concerning His great creative world. It is good that our minds and eyes should be stretched further out because I do not believe that at any point of the universe we get beyond the hand of God. Therefore, it helps us to understand the majesty of the Godhead when we begin to stretch our minds to reach out to the far corners of creation.

Lord TREFGARNE: My Lords, will the right reverend Prelate allow me to intervene? Is he actually offering ecclesiastical authority for the existence of another race of people in another universe? Is he saying that the existence of UFOs, together with their inhabitants such as are so often described to us, is compatible with Christian faith?

The Lord BISHOP of NORWICH: My Lords, I thank the noble Lord, Lord Tregfarne, for his interjection because it shows that he must have been listening carefully, because the next thing on my notes is, " Say something about Lord Trefgarne's remarks ". However, there are about 20 seconds to go before I get to the noble Lord. Perhaps in the meantime he can have a glass of water from Lord Davies of Leek, or something, but I am almost with the noble Lord. I am glad for that interjection because I obviously was not getting right what I was trying to say. I believe that all the far corners of the creative world, right out further than we can ever see or even know by radio, are

within the plan of the Creator. I believe
they are within the majestic purposes of
God. I believe that Christ, as Creator
under the Godhead, is concerned with it
all.

Now may I come to the noble Lord's
particular question a few mintues ago.
His question went something like this:
" Do we believe in the existence of another
race? Is it possible that there is another
race further affeld? " I must say that I do
not know. I believe there is a place for
reverent Christian agnosticism concerning
what is not revealed to us in scripture and
by our Lord. Having said that, I believe
that God may have other plans for other
worlds, but I believe that God's plan for
this world is Jesus. That at least is how I
view the question. The emphasis in
scripture is most interesting on the fact
that there never seems a point beyond
the revelation of scripture where there is
not God.

I quote, if I may follow Lord Trefgarne
once more before finishing what I had to
say, from the most majectic opening letter
to the Hebrews.

" In these last days, God has spoken to us by
his Son, whom he hath appointed heir of all
things, by whom also he made the worlds. He
reflects the glory of God. He bears the stamp of
his nature, upholding the universe by his word
of power ".

My point is that the danger of getting the
UFO thing linked with the religious thing
is that it obscures the fact that Christ is the
image of the invisible God, and that all
God's purposes and plans for humanity
are in and through his Son, our Lord.

This is not popular. This is not agreed
by dozens of people. Plenty of people

think that Christians make a proud and exclusive claim when they claim the words of our Lord,

" All power is given unto me in Heaven and in Earth ".

But this is part of the belief of a Christian which he has to put humbly and lovingly, and in the light of seeking to serve people. In the incarnation of our Blessed Lord he clearly revealed to us the mind of the Godhead, and we should be careful in our study of the UFOs in a religious context because I believe that the Gospel of Christ, and his death upon the Cross for the salvation of sinners, can never be by-passed by other forms of religious expression which may be esoteric, may be unusual, and may appear to come to us in unusual ways. For that reason therefore I am happy that we should make a cool, clear, careful study of the whole UFO situation, but let it not be at the price of the obscuring of the fullness of the Christian faith and its power to transform lives.

Viscount BARRINGTON: My Lords, before the right reverend Prelate sits down, may I ask one question? Although I agreed with much of what he said, I did not entirely understand, when he was telling us that one should not study UFOs in a religious context, whether that meant that one should not study music, art or other things that we all have, good, bad and indifferent, in a religious context. If it means that we must not worship them, then I would be entirely in agreement, as a professing Christian. We must not worship art, architecture, or music. But when he tells us not to study them in a religious context, I am not clear whether I will be doing so or not.

The Lord Bishop of NORWICH: My Lords, will the House give me permission to seek to answer that in a sentence? Just as it is important that the boys and girls in our schools today should know some basic facts about the great world religions, I still believe that it is essential that in a so-called and named Christian country our boys and girls should have the opportunity of knowing the great facts of the Christian faith. I am simply suggesting that, if, in fact, people seeking for religious experience bypass the revelation of God in Christ and revealed in scripture, then they may get into difficulties which will hurt and harm them. It is simply the obscuring of the Gospel that is my concern.

8.36 p.m.

Lord GLADWYN: My Lords, I must begin with an apology. Before I knew that the debate was to start so late I entered into an obligation for this evening from which I find it difficult to escape. Therefore, I may be unable to stay the course. One happy thing about UFOs is that they have nothing whatever to do with Party politics! Another is that they take one's mind off the absolutely frightful everyday events. Besides that, no theory as regards them can possibly be laughed out of court, nor need angels in respect of them fear to tread! I am sure that the noble Lord, Lord Davies of Leek, would agree.

Though many alleged sightings are of identifiable objects of terrestrial origin, such as disintegrating satellites, balloons or meteors, or even some sort of reflection, others are of things which, on the face of

LORD GLADWYN, 78, formerly Sir Gladwyn Jebb, was made a peer in 1960. He has had a distinguished career as a diplomat with appointments as Permanent Representative of the U.K. to the United Nations, 1950-54, and British Ambassador in Paris for six years to 1960. He was educated at Eton and Oxford, and speaks for the Liberal Party in the House of Lords. He is a notable champion of the cause of European unity, and has been active on many European committees and as a delegate to the Council of Europe. He lives in Suffolk and in 1979 became a candidate for election to the European Parliament.

it, cannot be accounted for in this way. The evidence of this is obviously too circumstantial to be disregarded. The evidence produced by the noble Earl, Lord Clancarty, and my noble friend Lord Kimberley, is obviously too circumstantial. You cannot disregard that. These things almost certainly do exist. It is difficult to say that they do not exist. Therefore, unlike the noble Lord, Lord Trefgarne, I do not contest their existence.

Some objects may be of terrestrial origin, but equally some may not. Whatever their origin, it has certainly not as yet been proved that they contain, or are controlled by, sentient beings of any sort. Still less has it been demonstrated that such sentient beings come from another planet, of which we are told there are many millions in the universe and no doubt many thousands on which conditions may well be similar to those on earth. It is conceivable, therefore, that UFOs come from another world; but that, to say the least, is not certain or, let us say, is not yet certain. Let us therefore for a moment examine the terrestrial and the non-terrestrial hypotheses.

If these objects are terrestrial, they come somewhere from our world, then they may conceivably be attributable to some condition of the atmosphere, or upper atmosphere, unknown to us, producing electrical or similar phenomena which no doubt interfere with compasses, and for some reason dart about the sky, sometimes even coming to earth. The difficulty about such an explanation is that they never seem to come into actual contact with aircraft, or any other air-

borne objects. Even if collisions have
sometimes been suspected, they have not
been proved to have occurred. Nor,
apparently, do they ever crash into
anything important on the ground. When
they are alleged to have been seen on the
ground it is always, incidentally, away
from houses. I suppose it is conceivable
that they may be capable of passing right
through physical objects, their mindless
trajectory being therefore harmless, and
dictated by some unknown physical cause,
and their apparent presence on the ground
being due to some local conditions on the
surface. All I say is that this is a conceivable hypothesis. In any case, the
fact that their occasional presence is so far
inexplicable does not in itself invalidate
the terrestrial hypothesis. There are, as
the noble Lord, Lord Davies of Leek,
said, more things in Heaven than are
dreamt of in our philosophy.

One terrestrial possibility at least can
be discarded, that which attributes them
to some Soviet activity in Central Asia,
in some way hearalding World War III.
This hypothesis was current, as I remember
well, in America at the time of the Korean
war, when I was in New York. Indeed,
it was responsible for, as far as I know,
the only known joke ever perpetrated by
a Soviet functionary, namely Mr.
Gromyko, who when asked what he
thought about flying saucers said, " Some
people say these objects are due to the
excessive consumption in the United
States of Scotch whisky. I say that is
not so. They are due to the activities of
a Soviet athlete, a discus thrower, in
Eastern Siberia, practising for the Olympic
Games and quite unconscious of his
strength."

If these objects are not terrestrial, then admittedly, always supposing they exist and are not mere illusions, they must be of some non-terrestrial origin. We can, I think, discard the possibility that they come from any of the other planets, as was said by the noble Viscount, Lord Oxfuird, whose maiden speech we so much appreciated; I hope we shall hear from him again shortly. Venus is too hot, Mars is a lifeless wilderness, and conditions on the others are extremely unlikely to be compatible with any form of life.

Thus, from whence do they come? They can only come from a planet in some other starry system, of which the nearest, as the noble Viscount said, is the star Proxima Centauri, which is $4\frac{1}{2}$ light years away. Always supposing, therefore, that UFOs are manned by sentient beings who travel at the speed of light—and if you travel at 186,000 miles a second, how do you slow down on approaching the earth? (how wonderful to imagine!)—these creatures must have been cooped up in their small machines for no less than 4·5 terrestrial years before appearing in our atmosphere. One can perhaps imagine that they may somehow have been able to escape from time and consequently not need any sustenance or sleep, but it is difficult, even on that hypothesis, to believe their machines are somehow time-exempt and can consequently contain enough propellant to keep them steady on their millennary way.

If a UFO was launched near Proxima Centauri and proceeded at the rate at which astronauts go to the moon, it would take, I am reliably informed, not

100,000 years but more like 900,000 years before it reached the earth. In which case, it is indisputable that any non-terrestrial UFO now sighted over New Zealand or anywhere else must have started on its journey something like a million years ago. In other words, since after all the human race lives within time, it must have left long before any kind of recognisable human society existed here below.

It is, however, also indisputable that UFOs have been observed for many hundreds of years in Europe, China and elsewhere. There are records of mediaeval monks seeing cigar-like objects in the heavens; and indeed it is quite possible that such sightings have been observed during the last few thousand years. There may be more sightings now simply because we have better facilities for observing them. If so, what conclusion must we draw as regards the whole non-terrestrial hypothesis? It is simply that these sentient and obviously highly intelligent beings from another planet, if such they be, at the end of an interminable journey, are content simply to hover about our atmosphere and not attempt a landing, or at least a landing of which we have any uncontrovertible evidence.

What could be the point of such strange proceedings? These sentient and obviously intelligent beings must have picked up enough information to conclude that a serious landing was feasible or, if not feasible, then to abandon the whole idea. Perhaps they may even in some mysterious way have been able to master our language and penetrate our thoughts. I think it was my noble friend Lord

Ancient and medieval accounts of strange aerial phenomena comparable to modern UFO sightings are quite numerous. Many have been explained as rare effects of nature, such as meteors, comets or displays of Northern lights. Others remain mysteries, like the "luminous cloud with a dome, like a hat" *(left of picture)* which was seen by six fishermen in 1656 hovering over the the church of St. Nicholas at Stralsund. It was followed by a mirage-like vision of a sea battle in the air. The case was officially but inconclusively investigated, and it was taken to have been an omen when fourteen years later the church was damaged by lightning. As in many UFO cases, several of the witnesses suffered physical or mental illness after the vision. From E. Francisci, *Der Wunder-reiche Uberzug unserer Nider-Welt,* 1620).)

Above: detail of the Nasca lines, with giant bird.

The Peruvian ground markings, referred to by Lord Gladwyn, are on the Nasca desert, where long, straight lines have been laid out across the landscape together with various symbols and representations of animals. They were formed by removing a layer of stones from the surface of the desert to expose the lighter coloured dust beneath. They are thought to have been made in about the 6th or 7th century A.D. by people of the vanished Nasca culture. Their purpose is still a complete mystery though Dr. Maria Reiche who has lived and worked among the lines for many years, believes that some of them were used in connection with astronomy to provide a seasonal calendar.

The suggested UFO connection arises from the fact that the Nasca designs can fully be appreciated only from the air. Lord Clancarty, following George Hunt Williamson, supposed that they were landing strips for extraterrestrial aircraft and this incredible notion was taken up and popularized by the opportunist UFO writer, Eric von Danicken.

In a recent book on Nasca, *Pathways to the Gods*, the explorer, Tony Morrison revealed the existence of other lines in South America, notably in the country of the Aymara people of Bolivia, who still tend and weed long, straight pathways through mountains and

Kimberley who said that conceivably they were under some sort of thought control from a planet in the neighbourhood of Proxima Centauri. If that is so and it is simply a question of thought control, then it comes down apparently to a sort of cosmic joke being played by these sentient beings from $4\frac{1}{2}$ light years away on the unfortunate inhabitants of this globe; they are a sort of hallucination in that they induce us by thought control to believe in them. It is a conceivable theory but I do not think it is a tenable one.

There are, it is true, those who believe that major landings from outer space have taken place in the past resulting in the inauguration of a new era, beings who then apparently withdrew after leaving behind some kind of representative, presumably to see how it would all work out; that is, the new civilisation which they had brought down to this world. In Colombia and Peru there are, I understand, strange markings on the ground thought to have been utilized by some sort of space ships, together with traditions of an other-wordly father of the race, notably of the Inca race, who came down from the sky. In fact, such traditions are fairly widespread in the world, although of course there is no proof that such father figures ever really descended from the sky.

The nearest one in time to our own era —I quote this only to draw attention to the lengths to which this kind of belief can go —is the theory, quite popular I believe in Russia, that Christ was a cosmonaut, the star of Bethlehem being a large UFO from which, to the amazement of the shepherds, emerged " the Heavenly Host " who left the babe in the manger, to the great benefit of all mankind, and then departed whence they came. You can believe such heretical imaginings if you will, and perhaps if you believe in the divine origin of Christ and his teachings it would not matter very much if you held that, in my view, rather non-sensical belief. And you can certainly believe, if you want, that UFOs contain people from another world which is watching us and whose intentions are benevolent and perhaps designed to save our distracted planet from the horrors of another war by somehow disposing of the wicked and thus inaugurating a new era. Believe that if you like.

I am afraid, however, that all such imaginings are due chiefly to the dis-content with the present human condition and to an unconscious desire to escape from the horrors or potential horrors of our earthly life. When we believed that if we were good we would, when we died, go to Heaven, there was no inclination to go to some new world near Andromeda; and whether another world other than Heaven itself was watching us did not worry us overmuch. Presumably, it was the angels.

The more over-populated our planet becomes, the greater the violence and the more appalling the wars, the more, unconsciously perhaps, we want to leave it if we can or trust in other worldly inter-vention; and the more intense therefore the longing, the greater the temptation to believe that there actually is somewhere else to which we can physically go or to which we can somehow make an appeal. It was a great disappointment when the moon was discovered to be a mass of grey plasticine, that Mars was even more

jungle which link straight rows of native shrines. This phenom-enon has evident similarities with the 'leys' of aligned sacred sites discovered in Britain.

unpleasant than the middle of the Sahara and that Venus was the nearest thing to Hell.

What is the moral? I agree with the right reverend Prelate, who said so eloquently—we are indebted to him for his intervention—that perhaps the moral is that we had better not put our trust in saucers for salvation but, rather, concentrate on how best to conduct ourselves here below so as to live in charity with our neighbours and eventually die in peace. If the UFOs contain sentient beings, we can only leave it to such being to get in touch with us when, and if, they will. Up to now, if they exist, they have done no harm of any kind. Apparently they have done no harm for the last two or three thousand years. So there seems to be no great need to set up intra-governmental machinery to investigate the whole phenomena. The mystery may suitably remain a mystery, and so far as I can see nobody will be in any way the worse off if it does.

8.50 p.m.

LORD KINGS NORTON, 76, was known before his creation as a life peer in 1965 as Sir Roxbee Cox. He is a former President of the Royal Institution, and a leading expert on aerodynamics, on which he writes and lectures. He has a particular interest in airships, and worked for five years as an engineer on the construction of the famous Airship R.101. He is married with two sons, and lives in retirement at Chipping Camden, Gloucestershire.

Lord KINGS NORTON: My Lords, I should like to add my thanks to those which the noble Earl, Lord Clancarty, has already received for opening the debate in such an extremely interesting way. I found my imagination boggling a little at some of the things he told us. Nevertheless, I feel that it is of immense value that this matter has been brought out into the open by the debate in the House, and I hope that as a result of it there will be some progress in the understanding of what is an extremely serious matter. I feel that we must be careful about our terminology in discussing the UFO problem, and I believe that I shall make clear in the course of my remarks what I mean by that. For example, in the past few days, since it was known to my friends that I was to take part in the debate, I have had over and over again the question: Do you believe in UFOs? I must say that I think that is rather a silly question, because if I saw something in the sky which neither I, nor whoever happened to be with me, could identify—I have not, but let us suppose that I did—then I should have seen an unidentified flying object, a UFO. I do not have to believe in it. I should believe merely that I had seen it—something that I could not explain; and I believe that many people are in that position.

It has been said more than once this evening that this is no new phenomenon. I think that the noble Earl, Lord Clancarty, dated it back to about 1300 BC. Whether my researches have taken me further back, I am not quite sure. However, I am sure that your Lordships will be as familiar as I am with the 10th Chapter of the Book of the Prophet Ezekiel. He certainly saw something very unfamilar in the firmament, and it certainly could be called a UFO. It was very different from the modern ones. It appears to have been coal-fired, to have been stabilised by gyroscopes, and crewed by cherubim; and it was a model which has not, so far as I know, been developed. There have been a good many sightings probably before Ezekiel, and certainly there have been many thousands since, and I fear that there has grown up a belief in many minds that if an object in the skies is unidentifiable,

Ezekiel's strange sighting is described in his tenth chapter. Featured in his ecstatic account are an object like a jewelled throne hovering over the Temple of Jerusalem and wheels which ascended into the sky. Two of the various interpretations of this version are here illustrated.

Lord Clancarty's book, *Mysterious Visitors,* firmly identifies the object of Ezekiel's vision as a spacecraft, and in *Spaceships of Ezekiel* Josef Blumrich, a space engineer with N.A.S.A., gives details of an inter-planetary flying wheel which he designed by following Ezekiel's description.

it must be from outer space; and this is quite unwarranted.

I think that it is worthwhile once again to consider the possibilities. I know that this has been done once or twice this evening, but it is part of my argument. I should say that there are possibly two kinds of objects to be seen in the skies: those of terrestrial origin, and those of extra-terrestrial origin. Typical of the first kind are man-made flying machines, satellites and rockets, and the like. Identifiable objects of the second kind are meteorites and phenomena such as the Northern Lights.

I am sure that many—and perhaps most—of the sightings recorded and reported are terrestrial in origin: aeroplanes with navigation lights glowing at night; satellite launching rockets burning up on re-entry; remotely piloted vehicles, now beginning to be called RPVs; up on trial flights; weather balloons; trick reflections of light. In the extra-terrestrial class I am afraid that I cannot think of anything other than meteorites, Northern Lights and ball lightning, but there are probably other well known physical phenomena within the knowledge of astronomers and meteorologists.

I feel, however, that some of the reports we have had—and we can for the time being leave out Ezekiel—are not readily explained in terms of any of the possibilities which I have mentioned. The New Zealand phenomena are worth much more investigation than they have yet had, but so far, in so far as I have been able to understand what has been reported, they do not appear to be explicable in terms of any of the suggestions which I have so far made. That seems to go for the quite extraordinary widespread sightings recently in Italy, where hundreds of people as reasonble as you and I, my Lords, seem to have seen quite inexplicable things in the sky. It would be worthwhile trying to explain them, and if there are people who know what they are, they ought to tell us. The high probability in my mind is that they are terrestrial in origin, and the only extra-terrestrial possibilities do not seem to be feasible because of the very eccentric paths which the objects, or lights, which were seen seem to have taken. But if they are terrestrial phenomena, we ought to be able to identify them.

I believe that any dispassionate investigation, such as I understand the noble Earl, Lord Clancarty, would wish to have, could not ignore the possibility of the phenomena having their origins outside the earth and perhaps outside the solar system. Just as meteorites are chance material projectiles originating in the solar system, may there not be random matter of a different character—perhaps a luminous but insubstantial character— that in certain circumstances becomes visible and attracted to our area? I certainly should be readier to accept some explanation in terms of what I might call the atsronomical phenomena than ships from outer space. It would, I suppose, be foolish to deny that possibility, but as an explanation of phenomena—and I think that the noble Lord, Lord Gladwyn, exposed this—it is surely a very long shot indeed.

If we are to conduct any dispassionate inquiry—and I think that we should—we must listen to the proponents of what one might call the *Star Trek* view. It can be argued, not unreasonably, that we in our humble way are probing nearby solar space with our Venus and Jupiter and other vehicular probes. We have ventured on to the Moon. Is it not presumptuous, the argument goes, to suppose that elsewhere in space creatures more advanced than us are probing into our space, probing with means now occasionally visible to us, using their own RPVs, controlled from stations light years away, rather on the lines which the noble Earl, Lord Kimberley, mentioned? It is a possibility which we must be prepared to consider. It is a possibility, though not many of us, I feel, would call it a probability.

But if we do have a study of UFOs, as the noble Earl desires, we could not exclude the possibility of extra-terrestrial intelligences from our consideration. This quotation has been given twice this evening, as well as a dozen times outside this House in this connection, but,

" There are more things in Heaven and Earth, Horatio ",

Hamlet said,

" than are dreamt of in your philosophy ".

And Heaven, my Lords, has always offered us more possibilities than earth. Although I remain sceptical of intelligent invasion from outer space, I recall the dictum of the late Mr. Sherlock Holmes when he was investigating the curious matter of the Sign of Four:

" When you have eliminated the impossible, whatever remains, however improbable, must be the truth ".

The desirability of getting rational and acceptable explanations for the odd phenomena which are being reported —even if, like some other para-normal phenomena, they are subjective—in my opinion is not, or should not be, merely to satisfy our curiosity. Here I am coming from rather a different angle to something which was discussed in greater depth by the right reverend Prelate the Bishop of Norwich.

There is a social danger, in my view, in leaving people in ignorance of the origins of these phenomena. I have recently learned from a number of sources that there have grown up, in North America particularly, many groups and cults whose attitudes are based on beliefs that UFOs are influential outer-spatial manifestations interested in this earth. In some cases these groups are looking to outer space for Man's salvation. If this is right, it is rather disturbing.

I find, too, that in this country there are groups interested, other than purely scientifically, in the UFO phenomena. I had a letter—and I think that other noble Lords may have had the same letter —earlier this week from an ecumenical Christian group which believes, among other things, that UFOs menace the spiritual health of the nation; that they are anti-Christian and that information exists about them which is being withheld. It seems to me that this association of UFOs with mysticism and religion makes explanation of the true origins of the phenomena a matter of great importance and of some urgency. The sooner that each reported sighting or landing is satisfactorily explained, the better. It is no good just laughing them off or trying to laugh them off; we must seek the truth and tell it.

My Lords, I remain sceptical, perhaps more sceptical than anyone who has spoken this evening except the noble Lord, Lord Trefgarne. I remain sceptical of the more bizarre extra-terrestrial explanations. I remain more than sceptical, indeed, incredulous, of what the noble Earl in his Motion called "landings"; but I support him wholeheartedly in his wish for a serious inquiry. I hope that the Government will take steps to put such an inquiry in hand. Finally, I come back to the matter of terminology. In his Motion, the noble Earl called for "an intra-governmental study". The noble Lord, Lord Trefgarne, and, I think, the noble Lord, Lord Gladwyn, took this to be an inter-governmental study. But "intra" means "within". I was puzzled by the use of the prefix, but that is what it means and presumably what the noble Earl meant. But why a study within the Government? I would support the idea of a Government-supported open investigation by a carefully chosen group of scientists and technologists with some funds at their disposal; but a study within Government would seem to smack of a secret probe, which would be no good at all.

I have no objection to a House of Lords study group, but they could scarcely perform in the way that a public organisation supported, say, by the learned societies and the engineering institutions could perform. It is something of that kind that I should like to see brought into being under Government or with Government support: a group of dispassionate people with the power, the money and staff on a modest scale to investigate. Perhaps in his reply later this evening the noble Lord, Lord Strabolgi, will comment on the suggestion.

9.4 p.m.

Lord RANKEILLOUR: My Lords, first, I must thank the noble Earl, Lord Clancarty, for this debate, the subject of which has long needed an airing; and, although the noble Viscount, Lord Oxfuird, is not in his seat, nevertheless I congratulate him on his speech. The UFO saga is deep and complex and there are no known experts to keep us up to date with everything to do with it including its mechanics. However, scientists throughout the world have been drawn into an ever-increasing discussion as to what UFOs are and where they come from, so far with little enough results except to wonder why the bounds of natural physics

LORD RANKEILLOUR was born in 1935 and succeeded his father in 1967. He went to the Roman Catholic school, Ampleworth, and now lives in Scotland, where his occupations are hunting, shooting, boating, genealogy and inventing agricultural machinery.

seem to be broken on all sides. Most Western Governments say that UFOs do not exist, but I think that the French Minister of Defence, M. Robert Galley, in February, 1974, said that they do; that his Government takes them seriously and that they have been studied secretly by a special department for over 20 years. Indeed, France leads the world in UFO research. It has followed up sightings with police teams, scientists and scholars and, since 1950, the *Deuxième Bureau* of the Army.

Oddly, in that same year, a remarkable report came from Farmington, New Mexico, on 18th March, when the inhabitants of that town were treated to a display of flying saucers that literally filled the sky above them. Every important American newspaper told the story. With few exceptions, the entire township of 5,000 people, including the mayor, newspapermen and members of the Highway Patrol, breathlessly watched an air show to end them all, a fantastic air circus. Countless saucers performed aerial acrobatics at speeds of 1,000 m.p.h. showing incredible handling, acute control in split-second timing by their ability to avoid collisions.

My Lords, that was hardly a weather ballon convention.

Is it not curious that we of the 20th century, with a vast knowledge of science behind us, should be blind to further wonders in the skies above? Men throughout the world have been branded as mad or mistaken when they have reported having seen strange sights in the heavens. Many men have seen these sights and have not been mistaken. Who are we to doubt their word? Who are Governments that dare to ridicule the honest? Not long ago the Loch Ness monster was regarded as a fable, but now our leading naturalist says that it (or they, possibly) probably exists. Why, then, should unidentified flying objects be any harder to believe, especially as they have been seen far more frequently? My Lords, of course they exist. Only a few weeks ago a Palermo policeman photographed one, and four Italian Navy officers aboard a light patrol boat in the Adriatic, in the early hours of the morning, saw a 300-yard long fiery craft rising from the sea and disappearing into the sky. Odd, strange, frightening, but apparently quite true. Indeed, why should these men of law enforcement and defence lie? Of course, they did not lie. Why should they; especially as in this case their sighting was backed up by men from a nearby radar station who saw it, too.

Each year there are many sightings of UFOs throughout the world. Some of them are very close at hand, while others are not, but always the effect upon those who see them is one of concern; and yet this very point is ignored and ridiculed by most Governments right around the globe. In the United Kingdom's case, those who report seeing UFOs are taken to be misinformed, misguided and rather below par in intelligence. If this is so, why has some of my information on this subject been given to me by the Ministry of Technology? Why should this Ministry waste its time gathering false information? Of course, it is not false information: it is data reported by civil and Air Force pilots, policemen, sailors and members of the general public who have all had personal experience which has intrigued and/or frightened them.

The naturalist referred to is Sir Peter Scott who, in December 1975, agreed that the much sighted but never captured Loch Ness monster should be allowed the dignity of a Latin name like any other creature of biology. The name chosen was *Nesseritas rhombopteryx*. Unfortunately for the dignity of the occasion, it was pointed out that the resounding title concealed an anagram – 'Monster hoax by Sir Peter S.'

My Lords, what are UFOs? I do not know; and nor, seemingly, do some Governments: but these machines do exist in one form or another, abstract or solid, and they do travel at stunning speeds which seem to defy proved natural physics. Let the United Kingdom be told by Her Majesty's Government the real details on UFOs so far as they know them, for by continued silence the position only becomes worse. Only a few weeks ago a UFO was seen near Kingussie, in the Highlands, and a few acres of Ashdown Forest were burned by another one. Is it safe to go on ignoring these appearances? Who is to know where they come from? But come they have. If we accept, then, that UFOs exist, we must next wonder how they operate. Their motive power would be of huge help to our transport and industrial life, for they apparently fly without wings at varying speeds from dead-slow to incredible ones, and even hover silently. This kind of information is above price, and therefore we as a country should make every effort to collect every scrap of information that we can. I therefore ask this Government to make the study of UFOs respectable by setting up a bureau that can be approached by all and sundry without any red tape or opposition, in an attempt to clear the air. Every sighting and landing must be thoroughly investigated by the bureau, in co-operation with the police, the Royal Air Force, the radar people and the British-based UFO investigators.

The noble Lord, Lord Strabolgi, who is to wind up this debate, is no doubt sympathetic to the reasons for these speeches, for it has become patently obvious to a great many people that this subject has got to the point when Governmental explanations must be forthcoming. A greater measure of open government is long overdue, and bringing the UFO saga into the realm of respectability would be one way of achieving this, in part. I suspect that the British Government do have a Department studying UFO sightings, for why else should they bother to go to such trouble to publicly debunk reported ones if they are of no interest to them? Quite apart from the fact that the Government have not admitted to the existence of UFOs, these machines are potentially dangerous. They give off blinding light, crippling rays and sometimes beams that immobilise humans; they start forest fires, eradicate crops and cause great distress to animals. If the British population was aware of this, they could sometimes take precautions. UFOs have been with us for many generations, so is it not about time that we officially recognised their existence and treated reports as less of a hot potato than hitherto?

Before the noble Earl, Lord Halsbury, takes me to task once again on the subject of sonic booms, I have one suggested answer to the question why these high-speed UFOs do not produce sonic booms. It is thought that these craft can produce a near vacuum envelope around themselves, which in turn would allow them virtually unlimited speed because they would thus be free of nearly all normal resistance, as they would be flying within it. Not being a scientist, I cannot enlarge upon this explanation, but I hope it is of some assistance to the noble Earl.

9.14 p.m.

Lord GAINFORD: My Lords, first

LORD GAINFORD, 57, went to Eton and Gordonstoun. He is a surveyor and geographer, and works as a local government officer for the GLC. He is married with two daughters, and his recreations are deer-stalking, cricket, golf, shooting, music, and antique aeroplanes may I add my congratulations to my noble friend Lord Oxfuird for his brilliant maiden speech. I hope that we are going to hear him many times again because it is quite obvious from what we have heard from him this evening that he is going to receive every possible encouragement to take part in many debates in the future. My main contribution to this debate is to assure the noble Earl, Lord Clancarty, of any support that I can give. If we are going to have a study group in your Lordships' House I shall be glad to be a volunteer to take part whenever I have the opportunity. I also thank him and others for initiating this debate, and for the pleasure of having such a refreshing subject to discuss in the midst of the present period of crices and strikes.

I am the 10th person to speak in this debate. I have noticed that so far none of your Lordships have actually reported a sighting, so here goes! I am going to stick my neck out, open my big mouth and trust I am not going to put my foot in it! I saw a UFO a little while ago. It was on 31st December about 8 p.m. All right, my Lords, have a good laugh, it was Hogmanay! Up in Argyll it was a New Year's Eve party and somebody said there was something funny flying across the sky. Fifteen of us came out to have a look, including some children. They had been drinking soft drinks anyway! The object was like a bright white ball with a touch of red followed by a white cone. In fact the whole object had the appearance of a small comet. It was heading eastwards and seemed rather low in the sky, passing over the hills between Loch Sweyne and Loch Fyne. The position from which we viewed it was outside the village of Tayvallich in Argyllshire on the West coast of Scotland about the same latitude as Glasgow.

As the ball disappeared into the distance it seemed to divide into two parts. It may have been a comet or a meteorite, but I should like to know what it really was. It would have been very beneficial if there had been some sort of centre to which I could write or telephone to report such an incident. No doubt setting up such an organisation would be an invitation to pranks, but for starting such a centre I suggest that volunteers could readily be found from the ranks of the former Civil Defence Service and/or the Royal Observer Corps. The Royal Observer Corps still exists but it has literally, if not metaphorically, gone underground where it is preparing to report and advise on nuclear fallout in the case of war. But there are many who used to serve it and who have not yet disappeared from the scene who could make valuable use of their past experience in establishing centres in various districts throughout the country—and I do not suggest that we start opening up the old observer posts in the countryside—to receive and analyse any reported sightings from the public. Such people with a sense of responsibility could, with a little experience, sift the genuine reports from the false.

Suggesting that such an organisation be set up, particularly at times like these, can naturally give rise to a protest about the waste of public money; but volunteers who might be willing to work for a few hours are quite prepared to do it for very small remuneration, if any at all. I have mentioned the Civil Defence Service, and

I did not know whether or not I should declare an interest, but I was a member of it during the 'sixties and I was one of many who were bitterly disappointed when it had to go into abeyance. I recall particularly the comradeship and the sense that we were doing a useful job for the community.

If I had the time and opportunity, I should enjoy volunteering for working in a UFO information centre, if that might be a suggested name for the organisation that would be required. I shall be interested to hear the summings up in this debate. I can give no explanation why there should be these phenomena concentrated within particularly the past 32 years as was confirmed by the noble Earl, Lord Clancarty, and these flying saucers in the year 1947 when the phrase was coined; but I would just accentuate what has been said before and add that if they are man-made or some astronomical feature, and provided there is no risk of any security breach, then the public have a right to know about them.

9.20 p.m.

THE EARL OF HALSBURY, 70, is an eminent scientist and Fellow of the Royal Society. He was educated at Eton, and has held many administrative posts in scientific education and as consultant to government, academic and business organizations. He is a former Governor of the BBC.

The Earl of HALSBURY: My Lords, in common with everyone else who has spoken, I should like to thank the noble Earl, Lord Clancarty, for giving us an opportunity to have, as it were, a scamper over the course and exchange views on this very interesting and controversial topic. At the same time, I should like to congratulate the noble Viscount on his maiden speech, which was obviously a very well thought out and well assemble set of considerations, which augurs well for his future in your Lordships' House, where I know he is already welcome.

At the risk of capping the stories of the noble Lord, Lord Gainford, I should like to tell your Lordships about some of the sightings I have seen. I will order them in terms of my *curriculum vitae*, beginning at the age of six, when I saw an angel. I do not know whether it was the noble Lord, Lord Davies of Leek, who mentioned angels, or whether it was the noble Lord, Lord Trefgarne, or the noble Earl, Lord Kimberley; but it is perfectly true that there was my guardian angel sitting on the edge of my bed. Naturally, with the imagination of a child, I clothed this presence in human form with a large pair of feathery wings. This presence proceeded to rebuke me for initiating a practice which it said would get me into trouble if I persisted in it. Having remembered the rebuke all my life and acted upon it, I am not prepared to deny the reality of the presence that was there with me. This should be a sufficient answer to the noble Earl—I see I have put him to flight—who thinks that if scientists come across something they cannot explain they are afflicted with a kind of vertigo. On the contrary, we welcome something we cannot explain because it is a new phenomenon which, as it were, stretches our capacities and brings out something in us.

The next item came along in year two of World War I. I was about eight years old, and the next thing that I sighted were Zeppelins. I used to go out after dark into the garden of the house where we lived and come back reporting the number of Zeppelins I had seen. What I had seen, in my interpretation of it, a Zeppelin—it was a large illuminated

Representation of a sundog as described by Lord Halsbury.

cigar-shaped object. In fact what I was looking at was the lenticular shape that the perspective of a searchlight thrown on to a cloud-base makes, and I was interpreting it as a Zeppelin and I was telling my parents how many Zeppelins I had seen.

The next one is sundogs and this fits very closely with what the noble Lord, Lord Davies of Leek, was saying about Macbeth's dagger and the laser holeographic reconstruction of things which really are not there. What sort of an interpretation would somebody who had never read about these or read about them put upon sundogs? Most people have not seen them or read about them. I was fortunate enough to have read about them and to have known the explanation before I saw the first.

When you look at a cloud with drops of water, you are looking at a diffuse reflection of the sun but if instead of there being drops of water in the cloud there are drops of ice, and if they were formed under meteorological conditions where all the facets of the crystals happen to be parallel as they fall through a rising stream so that they are remaining roughly stationary, the effect is of a rather dilute mirror, if one can so describe it. If the sun is up there, you see it actually reflected in this imaginary mirror down through the cloud, and one does not expect to see the sun looking down in this direction. Still less does one expect to perceive it travelling along beside one. Furthermore, one is not accustomed to focusing one's eyes on infinity in that particular direction. The only times it would be appropriate to do so would be if you were standing on top of a skyscraper where the vanishing point would be down here instead of over there, and it makes you rather dizzy.

Seeing a sky dog is a rather uncanny sort of phenomenon. You cannot focus on it properly; it does not seem to be anywhere in particular. It is flying along beside you—and what sort of terms would a person, who had never seen it before or read about it, report it in? I think that they would be rather bewildered. They might report it just as a child would report the vision of an angel as having human form and feathery wings. So it might easily be reported as anything that they had read about.

I now come to the green flash. I was about 20 and a student, and there was a controversy in the pages of *The Times* and in the correspondence columns of *Nature* about the green flash. What is it? Under certain rather rare atmospheric conditions, the last glim of the setting sun suddenly flashes brilliant emerald green. When I was a student 50 years ago, this phenomenon was not really established. It was possible to have a controversy as to whether there was such a phenomenon. People wrote to *The Times* saying that they had seen it. I remember one man who said that he had seen it when sitting by the shore off Bombay. It was eventually photographed during the International Geophysical Year, the IGY, some years ago.

However, before that I saw it myself in rather odd circumstances, after having read about it. I was bird watching in the far North-West of Scotland, by a sea loch called Loch Glencoul, near a little village called Drumbeg, where there is a cliff path. On that cliff path, there is a bench for the convenience of people who want to sit down and admire the view. Another traveller, a visitor to the district, was sitting upon the bench when I sat down and, by a chance coincidence, we were both using the same type of Hensholt binoculars and we got talking about our binoculars. There was a spectacular sunset, and when the sun was very low and it was safe to look at it through binoculars, I said to my fellow traveller, " Let us see if we can watch the green flash ". So we trained our binoculars and this very rare meteorological pheno-menon actually happened when I had just said to a fellow bird watcher, " Let us have a look to see if it happens " What would that person have made of it if I had not been there, just by chance, to tell him what the green flash was about?

Lastly, I come to ball lightning. I have never seen ball lightning, but the

Ball lightning, so called, is a rare and still mysterious phenomenon, and until quite recently there were scientists who refused to believe in its existence, attributing reports to optical illusions and so on. Its characteristic appearance is an amorphous floating lightball, which may enter rooms or enclosed spaces and explodes with a loud bang. At other times it appears in the open, and may even give the impression of chasing people, thus creating the popular notion that it is intelligently directed. In this it seems related to the UFO phenomenon, and there are many reports in the UFO literature of glowing balls swooping down onto cars, causing the engine to fail and terrifying the occupants, before taking off into the sky. Accounts of other strange lights, such as the will-o'-the-wisps and corpse candles of local tradition, have features in common with many ball-lightning and UFO reports.

Photographs of ball lightning are extremely rare, but the assertion that none exist is challenged by this picture taken at Basle Zoo in 1907.

description one reads of it is so coherent, so similar in all cases, that one must accept it as a phenomenon which occurs regularly in nature, though we cannot reproduce it in nature and attempts to reproduce it in the laboratory are, to my mind, unconvincing. There is no theory of it. It appears to take the form of a football-shaped mass of glowing gas which hops around or, if it has a chance, gets on to a conductor such as the rail in the gallery here and migrates along the conductor until it finally disappears with a bang. It has never been satisfactorily photographed, to my knowledge. If it has been, then the photograph must be a fairly recent one, and, as I say, it has not been reproduced. But this, again, should assure the noble Earl, Lord Kimberley, that, faced with an unknown phenomenon which I cannot explain, I do not get vertigo. I should be delighted to go ball lightning watching, as I go bird watching.

Lord DAVIES of LEEK: My Lords, may I ask the noble Earl one question? Has he ever seen a mirage? That is easily explicable, and one can also see it easily.

The Earl of HALSBURY: Yes, my Lords, and one can reproduce a mirage in the laboratory. You have a long tray of sand with bunsen burners underneath it, and you look at it from one end. It is quite a reproducible kind of phenomen. Science deals with material objects—things such as atoms and molecules; material processes—things such as the emission and absoption of radiation; and material forces—things such as the force fields which couple the objects to the processes. But if things are not material, then science has nothing to say. If you want to know what is the consciousness of a mind, I do not think science can either answer the question, on the one hand, or say whether it is a proper question, on the other hand. Therefore, from the scientific point of view, I can deal only with the assumption that these are material objects, and, if they are material objects, then, if they travel at the kind of speeds that are alleged, why do they not make supersonic bangs when travelling above Mach 1? The noble Lord, Lord Davies of Leek, made this point, and the noble Lord, Lord Rankeillour, also made it. I should like to go into the point in a little more depth.

We customarily express the speeds of

fast moving objects in terms of Mach numbers. Mach 1 is the speed of sound appropriate to temperature and pressure where the sound is being propagated. In terms of miles per hour, it is not a constant figure, but the advantage of using it as a parameter is that no matter what the temperature and pressure may be, Mach 1 is the speed at which the kinetic energy of a moving object—that is, the power to pack punch—is equal to its thermal energy. This is an unstable condition. The least disturbance to these unstable conditions entails the converison of kinetic energy into thermal energy with a bang, and this is what is called the shock wave. If one takes a cross section through a shock wave, there is a rise in pressure, temperature and entropy. There is complete discontinuity. That must happen when a material object is moving at Mach 1 or above through any medium.

The answer to the question put by the noble Lord, Lord Rankeillour—I have not had very long to think it out because he sprung it on me as a bit of a surprise—is this. If you were to create a vacuum, what would happen to the air you had displaced? Would you pull it in in front and push it out behind? If that is your means of travelling through the medium, you are merely moving some air backwards at the speed of sound, and it would create a supersonic bang just the same. Customarily, very often we hear two bangs because there is a bow wave and a stern wave from the moving object. Sometimes the bang degenerates into a rumble, just as a thunderclap degenerates into a rumble. Any noble Lords who have been uncomfortably close to a lightening bolt are aware that it makes a very pronounced

The item from the *New Scientist*, 18 January, 1979, is reproduced below. Note the the two incompatible explanations offered for the New Zealand UFO incidents.

Radar beams in on Kiwi UFOs. "Classic conditions" for false reflections of radar beams existed in the atmosphere over New Zealand on the nights that UFOs were spotted at the end of December, Christchurch meteorologist Dr. Neal Cherry has reported. UFOs were both spotted on radar and seen by an airline pilot, and a brilliant light was subsequently filmed by an airborne TV crew.

Dr. Cherry says that atmospheric conditions on both nights of the UFO sightings were "quite extreme". A thick band of cold, moist air lay over the sea with a dry, warm, northwesterly wind blowing over the top. Dr. Cherry theorises that the radar echoes reported by Wellington ground control were caused by atmospheric bending of radar beams, and that the visual sightings might have been caused by refraction of lights from a large squid fishing fleet that was at sea at the time. An experiment is being mounted to test this theory. An alternative theory is that the filmed object may have been Venus, which is particularly bright in the morning sky at the moment.

bang as the spark flies through the air.

If these are material objects and if they are moving at the speeds alleged, I cannot see them doing other than making a bang, so either they are not material objects or they are not moving at the speeds alleged, in which case the speeds are some kind of optical illusion. This throws doubt upon the rest of the reports that we received upon them.

In this week's *New Scientist*, published today, there is a report from New Zealand, and I should like to read to your Lordships a passage from it:

" Classic conditions for false reflections of radar beams "—

this tunes in very much with what the noble Lord, Lord Trefgarne, said—

" existed in the atmosphere over New Zealand on the nights that the UFOs were spotted at the end of December, Christchurch meteorologist, Dr. Neil Cherry, has reported. UFOs were both spotted on radar and seen by an airline pilot, and a brilliant light was subsequently filmed by an airborne TV crew ".

There is nothing in that report to suggest whether the optical sightings and the radar sightings came from the same point, or on the same alignment, or at the same time. We shall have to wait until the details become available.

I was much impressed by everything that the right reverend Prelate the Bishop of Norwich had to say on this matter and by some of the things which the noble Lord, Lord Davies of Leek, had to say, too. I do not think that anybody who reads the C. S. Lewis trilogy of space fiction, *Out of the Silent Planet, Perelandra*, and *That Hideous Strength*, will ever have his faith disturbed by doing so. C. S. Lewis, who was a profoundly Christian apologist, wrote the most marvellous space fiction of a complex universe, in which some of the created species were tempted and fallen, like ourselves; others were tempted and unfallen; and others were untempted. And they all had to live together in the same universe. I have always regarded the deeps of space and the immense time that it would take to travel from one inhabited world to another as being a kind of divine quarantine to prevent created beings from interfering with one another's cultures until they are civilised enough and mature enough to reach the point when they no longer want to do so. Too much of our science fiction is taken up with the supposition that vastly superior beings to ourselves are motivated by the same rather unworthy commercial motives as ours, and that they want to steal our coal mines or our water or set up imperialisms.

The little piece of fiction that I have always enjoyed most concerned a flying saucer which was hovering slowly in a circle round Central Park in New York and all the security forces turned out in order to do something about it. As it went round, it became more and more clear that it was going round in a spiral and not a circle and as the spiral grew smaller so the flying saucer grew smaller until it was very little more than the size of a waistcoat button going round the head of a maiden in New York Central Park. All the security forces converged on her because it was clear from the expression on her face that she was receiving a message, at which she smiled. Finally, the waistcoat button fell on to the path and was picked up and proved to be a waistcoat button and the security forces converged upon the maiden and bullied her into telling them—and she did not want to—what the flying saucer had told her. She said " I don't want to, because it will spoil it all." They said " Never mind, it may be very important for the security of the United States ". She said " Well all it said was ' Don't be unhappy; you are not the only lonely object in the universe'." I think that is a much more comforting thought with which to approach the subject of flying saucers than to suppose that they are engaged in some kind of imperialism.

Personally I have always believed, with the noble Lord, Lord Davies of Leek, in the Lochness monster. He is not the only person to believe in it. He was anticipated by Keats and I am quite sure that, when the poet wrote the line,

     " Thou still unravished bride of quietness ",

he must have had the monster in mind. Of course he did not go into it in great detail ; he did not tell us whether the monster was viviparous or oviparous. It may, of course, lay eggs, but if unravished, then infertile, and that is perhaps why there is only one of it. I have always thought that just as mother, when baking bread, leaves a little of the dough over in order that the children may make funny little men with raisins for tummy buttons and put them into ovens and bake them alongside the bread or the cake for the day, so possibly on the day of creation a little of the Divine creative power was left in reserve for the lesser cherubim and seraphim to use and they were allowed to make funny little objects like the Abominable Snowman and the Lochness monster, and therefore by the grace of

God since this is an orderly universe and a home is provided for everything, so the snows of Tibet were created for the benefit of the Yeti and Lochness was created for the monster.

Lord HEWLETT: My Lords, I join other noble Lords in congratulating the noble Viscount, Lord Oxfuird, upon his maiden speech but I run the terrible risk of being accused by the noble Lord, Lord Davies of Leek, of being an anthropological arrogant specimen. I am not quite sure what that means, and I am not quite sure that he knows what it means.

Lord DAVIES of LEEK: Oh!

Lord HEWLETT: All right, I am prepared to stand by it. I am only sorry to appear to be a veritable Daniel in a lions' den of UFO believers and to spoil the fun, and I have no doubt that today's flights of—dare I say it?—fancy will command far more attention than our debate yesterday upon British industry, which scarcely made today's Press at all. More's the pity. Of course, there is a danger in terminology and in gross assumptions. Many noble Lords have spoken as though UFOs were actually something, but of course we are precisely saying that if they are unidentified flying objects, we do not know what they are. So I quite agree, let us dismiss the concept of flying saucer equals UFO to start with. Let us try to take a slightly more scientific approach.

I would not dream of speaking in this debate had I not asked my very good friend and neighbour in the Cheshire

LORD HEWLETT, 55, was a Conservative peer and a former President of the Cambridge Union. He was a director of several chemical companies, and active in local politics and boy scout organizations in the Manchester area. On 2 July, 1979, Lord Hewlett, who had been ill for some time, was found with his throat cut at his home near Congleton, in Cheshire.

village of Swettenham, Sir Bernard Lovell, Fellow of the Royal Society and Nuffield Professor of Radio Astronomy, to be good enough to brief me at Manchester University Department of Radio Astronomy at Jodrell Bank, of which he is the Director. I went there two days ago and what I am about to say to your Lordships is based entirely upon that round table meeting with Sir Bernard and the members of his senior staff at Jodrell Bank. Of all the thousands of reports of sightings that have been made, whenever it has been possible to make an investigation they have been found to be natural phenomena, or in some instances, I regret to say, pure myth. Over the United Kingdom, Jodrell Bank's radio telescope, the first and still one of the most powerful in the world, has observed thousands of possible subjects for identification as UFOs, but not a single one has proved other than natural phenomena. I would ask the noble Earl, Lord Kimberley, to take the point on board. If UFOs, as he suggested, defy human knowledge, how do we really know by what possible means or possible background they even exist at all?

Let us get matters into perspective, my Lords, I beg you. At least 10,000 pieces of broken up rockets of American and Russian origin are known to exist in space and maybe there are many thousands more, and occasionally they do plough back into the atmosphere and burn up. Those must account, I think your Lordships would agree, for at least some of the so-called sightings of UFOs. Nature does provide fireballs, yes, meteorites, which bombard the earth at a rate of half a ton a day. Just take a tiny country like Holland. One hundred rocks the

size of your fist come through the atmosphere and hit that country in one year.
Consider Holland in relation to the size
of the whole of the world's surface and
you must surely realise that we are under
constant bombardment, not with UFOs
but with meteorites. A detailed study
on the Canadian prairies has displayed
how great is this bombardment which I
have just described over a wide area.
Even more staggering is the fact that it is
estimated that 8,000 million pieces of stone
and metal come to earth annually, many
of these burning up on arrival and these
give cause for these reports of unidentified
flying objects.

What is noticeable is the close correlation
between the position of the planet Venus
and the reports of UFOs, for when Venus
is low and bright in the sky and when it is
shining through thick mist or thin cloud
it does much more resemble something
other than our next door planet of the
solar system. Why, indeed, we are told
even the great President Carter has
spotted one, but it is a pity we did not
read the rest of the subsequent report.
It was later discovered that that was
Venus precisely in those conditions I
have described. If the great President
of the United States can be wrong, it is
just possible the few noble Lords remaining
in this House tonight might be, too. Let us
face it, we all would love to escape from
the miseries and frustrations of our world,
and particularly in these recent past days.
by all means go and see " Star Wars " or
" Jaws " or any other myth, but do not
confuse that with very serious scientific
study. That is carrying romance a little
too far. We must make sure we do not
make your Lordships' House a laughing

stock by doing so.

One of the most advanced experimental stations at Jodrell Bank—just take these statistics on board please, my Lords—has been on watch 24 hours a day for 30 years. Do you not think it reasonable for me to suggest that if there were UFOs at least one claim would have been made, but every single thing that has been seen and observed by radio astronomy has been identified as natural phenomena and as occurring from the universe itself as we know it—I do not say from the solar system; I say from our universe. If there were something in it—and the noble Earl, Lord Halsbury, is so right—of course the scientists would have been delighted to come forward with an announcement to that effect. After all, it was Jodrell Bank that managed to locate the Sputnik when the Russians, who so cleverly launched it, lost track of it in the atmosphere. So do not think that this is some denigrating comment by the scientific lobby and some nasty, cheap debunking exercise. No, my Lords. We must take a serious scientific view of the actual surveys and of what has been discovered.

Lord DAVIES of LEEK: My Lords, I am delighted to hear what the noble Lord says. However, I beg the noble Lord to remember that there are other scientists who say that of course we know that there are meteorites—there have been for the whole of time—but there are some factors outside that range which justify (and this is all we ask) an attempt at identification. There is no difficulty in identifying meteorites. We are not asking for that: we are asking for the identification of other types of phenomena.

Lord HEWLETT: My Lords, that promptly begs the question. That is precisely what I am saying. The identifications that have been made are not necessarily of individual meteorites: they are of endemic portions of rockets and so on. During 30 years study and a constant watch for 24 hours a day there has been not a single sighting of any description which could possibly or remotely be considered worthy of serious study as a UFO. Every single thing has been explicable. With all respect, it is no use noble Lords saying that this is not a convenient answer: we must find some things that are not explicable. I am telling your Lordships and it is perfectly fair. Your Lordships may say " Scientists ". I am quoting one of the leading world, radio astronomers—indeed, probably the leading world radio astronomer. Frankly, scientists can be anything from a B.Sc. London University, passed yesterday. However, I am talking about 30 years experience of radio astronomy and a professorship of the highest standing and order in the whole world. Both the United States and the Soviet Union come to Sir Bernard at Jodrell Bank for assistance.

Lord DAVIES of LEEK: My Lords, nobody is denigrating what the noble Lord is saying, but he is off beat here. All we are saying is that there are some of these phenomena that need investigation—that is all.

Lord HEWLETT: My Lords, perhaps the noble Lord could show me just one phenomenon which requires ——I have

The assertion that professional astronomers never see UFOs is often made by de-bunkers of the phenomenon. However, the facts prove otherwise. A report by Dr. Peter Sturrock of Stanford University in 1976 on his survey of astronomers' UFO experiences is summarized by James Oberg in *Omni*, February 1979. Of the 2,611 astronomers polled, 70 replied that they had "witnessed or obtained an instrumental record of an event which I could not identify and which may be related to the UFO phenomenon."

Several astronomers admitted to having witnessed characteristic UFO effects, such as unexplained lights or luminous objects hovering, making instantaneous turns or moving in formations, and there were other more dramatic sightings, including as "flying platform complete with rotating radar antenna" which appeared low over the campus at Princeton one evening in 1969.

Ufologists point out that astronomers, who scan remote, very limited areas of the sky, are unlikely to observe aerial phenomena close to earth. It may also be true that a promising young astronomer who wishes to remain promising would be unwise to report UFO sightings among his professional colleagues.

given way a good number of times and I should be grateful if the noble Lord would let me finish my sentence. I am saying that Jodrell Bank, which covers the whole of the United Kingdom, has been on watch for 30 years. It is probably the most powerful radio telescope in the world. With great respect, if it has found nothing whatsoever to report in a positive way then, for the noble Lord, Lord Davies of Leek, to throw at me, " some scientists think that . . . " is not good enough.

Lord DAVIES of LEEK: My Lords, we must not take more time.

Lord HEWLETT: No my Lords, we must not, so I fear that the noble Lord must give way to the argument. I shall give way to the noble Earl Lord Kimberley. I knew that I should have a rough time!

The Earl of KIMBERLEY: My Lords, does the noble Lord not think it conceivable that Jodrell Bank says that there are no UFOs because that is what it has been told to say?

Lord HEWLETT: I certainly think it inconceivable—absolutely and completely inconceivable. I have known this scientist personally for more than 30 years. I would not dream of going along for a briefing, so to speak, on the estimation that he was to con me or that I was some tool of the CIA to kid your Lordships. Please do not let us carry this fantasy too far. I shall deal with one or two other aspects of the noble Earl's speech and then he shall see some correlation to the whole of my argument.

Let us turn to the defence interests of

the Pentagon and other Western defence establishments. When they have been challenged they have refused to say that UFOs do not exist. Nor have they said that UFOs do exist. They are not committed. We are all men of the world and frankly there are advantages in making an international over-estimate of the possible potential strength of one's potential enemy and his ability to combat one in sectors in which one cannot adequately reply. I think that it would be most unwise of any defence establishment to make a categorical denial of UFOs, and equally foolish of me to do so. I am not trying to prove the existence of nothing or that something does not exist. I am saying that in the scientific evidence so far—and I can deal only in detail with the United Kingdom—there is no evidence whatever from the greatest radio telescope of a single UFO. I think that the attitudes of defence establishments worldwide, even including the Soviet Union, are probably wise: they must display the antithesis of over-confidence and complacency, lest there should perchance be some new arm of warfare that they have not adequately explored or even entered. Particularly did this attitude apply in the first decade after the Second World War when, frankly, the start of the " cold war " and the intense fear of the Soviet Union's possible aggression against the West when we were the sole possessors of atomic weapons, must have provoked such a degree of intense interest in the possibility of a new arm of warfare.

I am sorry that the right reverend Prelate the Bishop of Norwich is not here, but I am glad that the noble Lord, Lord Trefgarne, is on the Opposition

Front Bench. I quote from Sir Bernard:

" Whether we are the only people in the universe is entirely another matter. That is a subject of very serious importance and is being investigated ".

But there is no direct connection between the possibility of other persons occupying other bodies, either within or outside our own solar system. However, one thing is quite clear: there is an infinitesimal chance that there exists other people who could be within our time-frame—and I refer of course to the statements made by the noble Lord, Lord Gladwyn, and the noble Earl, Lord Halsbury—who would be able to spend perhaps ten or hundreds of light years getting here and who would have survived that length of time in those atrocious conditions and entered our earth atmosphere assuming that they are some sort of humanity and have some form of flying saucer, or whatever our friends proclaim it is. How could they possibly meet us in those circumstances? Let us take the million-to-one possibility that they could. Do your Lordships mean to tell me that they could get so close to us as to be sighted, but be incapable of any form of communication or identification whatever? No, I am sorry.

I have listened most carefully to everything that has been said. The noble Earls, Lord Clancarty and Lord Kimberley, have claimed sightings from times before Christ, through the Middle Ages up to the present day. Those noble Earls know full well that the amount of scientific knowledge in the Middle Ages, and particularly before the times of Christ, simply did not allow a tenable theory that they had that degree of knowledge to be able to understand any of the phenomena that we know today. Indeed, in the last 30 years there has been a dramatic change in the sum total of knowledge in this field. No doubt that is why Jodrell Bank can proclaim that they have had no evidence of sightings of any description which are not perfectly explicable as natural phenomena within our own universe.

I am sorry, the existence of UFOs is even more fanciful than Gilbert and Sullivan's Iolanthe—charming indeed, but I am afraid a joke upon your Lordships' House. I am afraid that some of my noble friends join the flat-earthers, who will make the best playmates for this particular lobby. We have a duty to the country to explode the myth. Tonight we have been carried away in realms of fascination and delight, but they have precious little to do with the facts. I suggest that the myth must be exploded. We must return to work in this dreary old world and the difficulties we are in. But I beg your Lordships, and in particular the noble Lord, Lord Strabolgi, for heavens' sake, no more Government Departments of inquiries. That alone we should be spared as the result of this excellent debate.

9.55 p.m.

The Earl of CORK and ORRERY: My Lords, I hope that the noble Earl, Lord Clancarty, will not be cast down by the speech to which he has just listened. I myself must confess that I know remarkably little about unidentified flying objects. I know a few things about them. I know quite a bit, and I have learned more since the beginning of this debate, about attitudes towards them. They are almost as interesting in some ways. There

THE EARL OF CORK AND ORRERY, 68, was educated at Harrow and Sandhurst, and served as a regular officer with the Royal Ulster Rifles. During the war he fought with the Parachute Regiment, and with the Chindits in the jungle where he was severely wounded. He is now an artist, broadcaster and author, and interests include sailing (one of his publications is *Sailing in a Nutshell*, 1935) and gardening. He lives in Sussex.

is one type of attitude towards them that I view with respect, and that is the attitude represented by people who call themselves, or perhaps to be fair are called by others, " ufologists ". I do not know whether the noble Earl will accept that word. I rather hope he would not.

I admit the charm, the satisfaction, and the neatness of UFO as—this is the word the noble Lord, Lord Davies of Leek, is so good at—an acronym, coming from " unidentified flying object ". But it unfortunately leads to a word which to disrespectful persons, and there are some about, might be suspected as originating somewhere between illiteracy and the purely silly; rather as though a keen student of the affairs of the United Nations should describe himself as a " Unologist ", and his interest " Unology ". That would have been severely distressing to my late lamented friend Lord Conesford, and indeed to me.

If there is an agency set up for collecting and correlation of information, as I hope there will be, I suppose it could be called " Ufo info ", which would have a certain elfin charm. But I am admittedly being absurd, and being so on purpose. I am doing it for defensive reasons, and I hope that the noble Earl will not think that I am being offensive. I am not. I hope that somebody will think of a better word. There is in fact a Greek word " *téras* ", meaning a portent in the sense of a marvel or wonder, which would generate quite nicely a teratologist, or teratology. In fact I am not sure that teratology is not in the dictionary as the study of monsters. It is not a word that is widely used. It is not on everyone's lips very often, and it would not really matter if it were taken over to refer to portents. There is a precedent for this kind of thing, in television. As noble Lords will know, television originally meant, before it meant what it means now in the familiar sense as we understand it, clairvoyance, and nobody finds any confusion now. Whatever it may be known as, let us proceed and not waste time.

I must make a remark—nobody has done so so far, I suspect rather to his surprise—about the speech of my noble friend Lord Trefgarne. If he had been speaking as a private Back-Bencher I would probably have not said anything, but he was speaking from the Dispatch Box. Therefore, he presumably represents the views of the Party to which I belong. It is a view I wish to disown entirely, because if a Party of any magnitude cannot produce better views than that on a serious subject, I confess I am ashamed of it. If this represents all that the Conservative Party can produce in the way of thinking on what is undoubtedly a serious subject, whatever your opinion about it may be, then this is deplorable.

If the noble Lord really thinks that there is no serious interest or belief taken nowadays in witchcraft, perhaps he does not read the right newspapers, but I can assure him that this is far from true. He is not a believer in unidentified flying objects. " I am no believer in UFOs ", he said. I do not know how you can not believe in UFOs. You can take it for granted, if your mind takes a leap ahead, that by an unidentified flying object something is intended that is supposed to have originated in outer space, and you can say you do not believe in that. But I do not know what it implies to say that you do not believe in an unidentified flying object. You do not believe in the object? You do not believe in its flying? You do not believe it is unidentified? There are things that are unidentified. Perhaps we are not trying. I do not think it is reasonable to say that they do not exist. Nobody, except my noble friend Lord Hewlett, has seriously contended that they do not exist. The question is, what are they?

Lord TREFGARNE: I am pleased my noble friend has allowed me to intervene, my Lords, because he has been very caustic about what I had to say. I do not deny the existence of unidentified flying objects. I simply say that most of them are identifiable, that some are not objects at all but simply a trick of the light or a meteorological phenonemon—I think that is so in many cases—and that I agree one cannot deny the existence of unidentified flying objects. It is simply a question of how we identify them.

The Earl of CORK and ORRERY: My Lords, I take my noble friend's point. I am anxious not to misquote him, but he also said that ufologists—it is difficult not to use that word—referred to unexplained sightings which would be explained if only we had better evidence; that was the gist of one part of my noble friend's argument. In other words, if we had better evidence we should be able to explain those sightings. That is the sole point on which the noble Earl initiated this debate. That is what he is asking for:

he wishes evidence to be collected, collated, examined, evaluated and reported on as to what these things are, and it is notable that he himself did not say what he thought they were. Other noble Lords have spoken as though he had said they were fairies or I do not know what, when in fact he said no such thing. I believe he is a leading authority on these matters— certainly he has studied them more closely than anyone else of whom I have heard— and he must have exercised very great restraint in this matter, and he is to be congratulated on that as well as on initiating the whole debate.

I once had an ancestor—I still have him in a sense, in that he is still my ancestor although he is dead—called Robert Boyle who founded a society called the Royal Society. I feel that if he returned to the rooms of that enormously prestigious society now and found that the present Royal Society contained Fellows of such erudition and charm as the noble Earl, Lord Halsbury, he would feel entirely at home; a man of the most agreeable and totally non-sceptical nature, even if he did write a book called *The Sceptical Chemist*.

The noble Earl has done a service by displaying before our very eyes the scientist-philosopher who knows precisely the limits of science and makes no effort to go beyond them. Nor does he point the finger of scorn at anyone else. He must know, as others know, that it is impossible to prove anything by negative evidence. If you wish to prove that something is not so you can do it only in logic—by proving the existence of something that is so that makes that first premise impossible. Thus, you cannot prove that any particular type of flying object does not exist, and with respect to my noble friend, the fact that the Jodrell Bank telescope has not seen something not only does not prove, but is not even particularly good evidence, that it was not there. I am prepared to accept, if told, that the Jodrell Bank telescope has been operating on a frequency suited to the observation of UFOs of one kind or another for the last 30 years, but, until I am told that, I shall be sceptical in that matter.

Lord HEWLETT: Let me be quite clear about this, my Lords. I did not say other than that Jodrell Bank had made many thousands of sightings but had been able adequately to explain them away as natural phenomena from our own universe.

The Earl of CORK and ORRERY: I thought that I had my noble friend right, my Lords; in other words, the telescope has not seen anything that was inexplicable. But I do not think that that is really an argument that something does not exist. The question is: what kind of thing can it be? I hope that my noble friend does not think that I am going on about him—I no longer am. How is it possible to maintain more than a certain degree of doubt in 1979?

I remember, as may some other noble Lords, one or two of whom may be present in the Chamber, my predecessor who sat in this House. He was born in the year 1886. When he was born there were no motor-bicycles or gramophones, fountain pens, safety razors or electric trains. Messrs. Daimler and Benz in Germany were just putting the first petrol-driven car on to the road, and Einstein, I think, was eight years old. My noble and gallant kinsman, when he finally left the active list of the Navy at a very advanced age, had lived into the age of the nuclear submarine, having begun his first sea-going voyage under sail. That was the band of progress represented technologically in the lifetime of one serving naval officer. What would he have said had he been told that in my lieftime—and I am not even all that near the end of it, either—I should see men on the moon; or computer technology carried to the pitch that it has reached; or that there would be such an outbreak of wisdom following Einstein and men like Schrodinger, Heisenberg and others; or the astonishing ascent of knowledge into the atomic world?

This has all happened in the lifetime of many of us, and yet we sit here, some of us, and say that marvels which have been postulated by some, and which indeed are less in magnitude than most of those would have been to my uncle, are impossible. We are not all saying that—perhaps nobody is saying that—but the argument is quite untenable. I have no wish to express any view on what a UFO may be. What I wish to say is that there is no knowing what it is not. It may be a product of some kind of sign language, as the noble Earl, Lord Kimberley, mentioned. It may be mechanical. It may be purely terrestrial. I doubt if it is angels. But I believe that, for the clearing up of mystery, for the removal of doubt, for even the eliminating of some of the dangers which may exist and to which the right reverend Prelate referred, some kind of an open inquiry ought to be set up. I am rather inclined to agree with the noble Lord—I think that it was the noble

Lord, Lord Kings Norton—who said that probably it should not be an intragovernmental inquiry. I think it should be someting rather more open than that, but it ought to take place. If a group is set up within this House, as suggested by the noble Earl himself, that would be excellent. I should myelf be entirely in favour of it. In any case, let us get this matter cleared up and into the open, and by all means let us take it seriously, because this is a serious subject. Far too many people are taking it seriously for it not to be a serious subject.

Finally, I wish to voice my most sincere congratulations to my noble friend who made his maiden speech this afternoon. It is very impertinent of me to congratulte him upon it, but I should like to say how much I enjoyed it. I have not yet said anything complimentary about the noble Earl who initiated the debate. I have left this to the end on purpose because I think it may not be entirely realised what a service he has done. This is the first such debate that has occurred in any society such as this particular one; and this society, by which I mean this noble House of Parliament, is probably the only legislative assembly in the world in which it could happen. I hope that it will have repercussions which will spread far beyond this Chamber. What the outcome will be I do not know, but, in initiating the ripples which I hope will spread all over the surface of the mill-pond, the noble Earl has done a most valuable service.

10.10 p.m.

Lord STRABOLGI: My Lords, I should like to join with the noble Earl,

LORD STRABOLGI, succeeded to one of the oldest English titles, created in 1318. He is a member of the Fabian Society and an active Labour Party politician. At the time of the debates he was Captain of the Yeoman of the Guard (Deputy Chief Whip), and his interests include the arts and Franco-British relations.

Lord Cork and Orrery, in saying how grateful we are to the noble Earl, Lord Clancarty, for initiating this debate on UFOs. Of course, the subject has been of considerable interest in this country, and I hope our discussions, which, as the noble Earl rightly said, have been the first that we have had in your Lordships' House, will help to increase public understanding. But before I reply in detail to the debate—and I think it has been a most interesting one—I should like to join with my noble friend Lord Davies of Leek in congratulating the noble Viscount, Lord Oxfuird, on his maiden speech. We were very glad to hear from him, if I may say so, and I hope we shall hear from him again on many other occasions. I shall be referring to some of the detail of his speech later, but at this stage I should like to offer him my warmest congratulations.

There are undoubtedly many strange phenomena in the skies, and it can be readily accepted that most UFO reports are made by calm and responsible people. However, there are generally straightforward explanations to account for the phenomena, as I think was said by the noble Lord, Lord Trefgarne, speaking for the Opposition—and I must say that I welcomed his constructive speech. There is nothing to convince the Government that there has ever been a single visit by an alien space craft, let alone the numbers of visits which the noble Earl, Lord Clancarty, claims are increasing all the time. As has been said today, we live in a huge universe. I find as awe-inspiring as Pascal did the contemplation of infinite space. There are some 100,000 million stars in our galaxy alone, which it would

take 100,000 years to cross at the speed
of light. Beyond our own galaxy, the
distances become even more daunting.
The light year, as your Lordships know,
is about 6 million million miles. The
Andromeda galaxy is over 2 million light
years away, and that is in our own local
group of galaxies! There are, of course,
other groups as well.

The evidence suggests that there is no
intelligent life on the other planets of
our own solar system, as the noble Viscount said. There are, of course, different
views about whether there might be life
elsewhere in the universe, but certainly
there is no serious positive evidence to
show that there is. If there were an
advanced civilisation elsewhere in the
universe, as my noble friend Lord Davies
of Leek supposed, with the technology
to traverse these colossal distances, there
are many questions to be answered. What
is the point of this alleged huge number
of visits to our planet, over three decades
or more, to no apparent purpose? There
seem to be internal inconsistencies in the
idea. To put it simply, if these alleged
aliens prefer to keep out of the way, the
number of reported sightings would surely
be only a tiny portion of the actual UFO
movements, which would run into many
millions. If they do not prefer to pass
unnoticed, we could surely expect un-
mistakeable appearances.

Why have they never tried to communi-
cate with us? Why has there been no
evidence on radio of attempts at communication? And would not such a
large number of movements be picked
up by our defence radar system? Why
has not a single artefact been found?
Assuming that each visit does not repre-

sent a journey from a distant star, where are these alien space craft supposed to be hiding? Now that the idea of such bases on the moon or on another planet in our solar system is barely tenable, ufologists have had to claim that the aliens are based in the depths of the sea or in a great hole in the earth, or even that they come from invisible universes and other space-time continua. Anyone who accepts the hypothesis of large numbers of alien visitations seems forced towards explanations that are ever more fantastic, and incapable of either proof or disproof.

As I have said, there really are many remarkable things to see in the sky; and most UFO reports relate to actual phenomena reported by sensible people. But, my Lords, let us consider the phenomena themselves—and the noble Lord, Lord Trefgarne, mentioned some of these. Huge quantities of space debris enter our atmosphere, and are often seen as meteors, and fireballs; bright planets and even the moon or stars have been reported as UFOs, in unusual atmospheric conditions, as the noble Lord, Lord Hewlett, said; there are tricks of light on cloud, and particular cloud structures; there is Aurora Borealis, St. Elmo's Fire and ball lightning which was referred to by the noble Earl, Lord Halsbury, which has been known to drift along telephone or power lines. There are some 5,000 man-made objects in orbit, satellites and debris, some of which can be seen by the naked eye, some through binoculars. About 600 such man-made objects re-enter the atmosphere every year, as the noble Lord, Lord Hewlett, reminded us. The quantity is far less than natural space debris, but, my Lords, the phenomena can be astonishing.

Last April the Ministry of Defence received reports of a large piece of debris re-entering across the South of England. Most reports were factual, but one spoke of an

". . . oval thing with a white cockpit which hovered for a while then shot off at great speed ".

My Lords, we cannot prove that this was not a UFO, but it occurred at the same time and place as known re-entry of debris.

Many reports relate to aircraft seen in unusual conditions at unusual angles. One recent UFO was confidently reported on local radio. Again, my Lords, we cannot prove that it was not a UFO, but we do know that an RAF Vulcan bomber on a low-flying mission passed the same spot at the same time and on the same course as the reported UFO. Aircraft lights have led to UFO reports; as have distant aircraft with landing lights on— I have seen them myself—flares from aircraft, short condensation trails lit by the sun after dusk and light reflected from aircraft. Other phenomena include meteorological balloons. The Meteorological Office alone releases 50 such balloons every day, which expand to 40 ft. in diameter and rise to 100,000 ft. and can be lit by the sun after dark. Many other organisations, such as universities, use balloons, some much larger. Meteorological searchlights shine on clouds: the beam itself cannot be seen; only a point of light in the sky. There are hot air balloons and kites; even birds have been reported as UFOs; lights on distant towers; car headlights on distant hills; dust devils; and airborne debris carried by the wind.

All these phenomena can be misinterpreted by the most sensible observers, particularly when seen unexpectedly and briefly and in unusual atmospheric conditions. This is what opponents of the natural explanations forget. With distortions of light, and mirages, the most commonplace things can be so changed as to be barely recognisable. For instance, I am told that the US Air Force attributed the 1947 sighting by Arnold described by the noble Earl, Lord Clancarty, to a mirage effect.

Phenomena seen through glass are suspect. There are phenomena generated within the eyeball and there are optical illusions to which the noble Earl, Lord Halsbury referred. One scientist, whose task includes watching satellites, describes how, when observing stars near moving clouds, he finds it difficult to escape the illusion that the stars are flying past stationary clouds. The noble Earl, Lord Halsbury, referred to the green flash. I used to see it myself in Alexandria when on leave. It was one of our evening pastimes to sit on the promenade and watch it go down over the sea.

My Lords, in 1968, the United States Air Force commissioned the University of Colorado to carry out an independent study into UFO phenomena. Their report, which was published in 1969, was very substantial and detailed and it covered some 50 examples of such phenomena, but added that it was impossible and potentially misleading to try to tabulate all of the possible causes of UFO perception: there are simply too many. The report's main conclusion was, and I quote:

On 6 October 1966 the University of Colorado set up a project for UFO investigations at the request of the U.S. Air Force. It was called the **Condon Committee** after its director, Dr. Edward U. Condon, a senior military scientist. The evident purpose behind the formation of the Committee was to calm public anxiety about the extent and unknown quality of the UFO phenomenon, and this was clearly expressed in a memorandum addressed to the University at the very start of the project by Robert J. Low, the project co-ordinator. Part of this reads:

"Our study would be conducted almost exclusively by non-believers who, although they could not possibly *prove* a negative result, could and probably would add an impressive body of evidence that there is no reality to the observations. The trick would be, I think to describe the project so that, to the public, it would appear a totally objective study but, to the scientific community, would present the image of a group of non-believers trying their best to be "objective" but having an almost zero expectation of finding a saucer."

One of Dr. Condon's earliest statements on his UFO inquiry was:"My attitude right now is that there's nothing in it."

Even among the 'non-believing' scientists on the Committee there were several who accused Condon early on in the project of being less than objective in his treatment of the UFO evidence. Two of them, Dr. Norman Levine and Dr. David Saunders, were fired from the Committee for making such criticisms, and the latter went on to write a book, *UFOs?Yes!*, which exposed Condon's objects and methods, showing, for instance, how Condon emphasised 'crackpot' UFO reports while ignoring or playing down the more serious evidence.

The Condon Report of 1969, was a masterpiece of obfuscation. Buried within the 965 turgid pages of its paperback edition *(Bantam Press)*, were details of a mere 960 UFO cases investigated, a third of which were admitted to be unexplained. Few journalists had time to read through the entire report and note the remarkable evidence concealed within it, and press comment was almost entirely based on Dr. Condon's 'summary', which failed to mention the unexplained aspects of his cases, and left casual readers with the impression that the UFO rumours had been thoroughly and dispassionately investigated and proved to be without foundation. Most comm-

" Nothing has come from the study of UFOs in the past 21 years that has added to scientific knowledge ".

The findings of this report were endorsed by a panel of the National Academy of Sciences.

There really are tens of thousands of strange things to be seen. It is the custom to call such phenomena " UFOs ", and to transpose this easily into " alien space craft ". Often the appearance is too fleeting and the description too imprecise for a particular cause to be attributed. What we can say is that there is a great variety of plain explanations. There is no need, I suggest, for the far-fetched hypothesis of alien space craft.

To genuine sightings we must, however, add hallucinations; the excited tales of the gullible; and the embellishments of the born romantic. There are also indications that ufologists accept reports of UFOs somewhat uncritically. The noble Earl, Lord Clancarty, referred to a papyrus found among the papers of a Professor Tulli recording flying saucers during the reign of Thutmose III. The Colorado Report, which I mentioned earlier, inquired into this story. The alleged papyrus could not be traced, but internal evidence in the translation suggested a fake; inquiries with the Vatican Museum also suggested that Tulli, an amateur Egyptologist, had been taken in by a fake.

There is a category of UFO cases which are difficult to explain because the description is too vague or the evidence too remote, coupled perhaps with a coincidence of different phenomena and with exceptional conditions. If one accepts that there are natual explanations that could account for most sightings, it is an enormous and irrational jump to claim that the residue of difficult cases constitute alien space craft when there is no positive evidence that they do constitute alien space craft.

I should mention the famous UFO reported over the United Kingdom in December 1978, on New Year's Eve in fact. This was the one probably seen by the noble Lord, Lord Gainford, to which he referred. The phenomenon was probably the re-entry of a launcher associated with the Russian space satellite COSMOS 1068, launched on 26th December. Of over 100 reports reaching the Ministry of Defence, nearly all were factual and consistent with the re-entry of satellite debris.

The recent sightings in New Zealand referred to by the noble Lord, Lord Kings Norton, attracted worldwide publicity, and we understand that the New Zealand Government may make an announcement when the facts have been assembled and appraised. Preliminary advice from our High Commission in New Zealand shows confident expectation that the sightings will prove to be due to natural phenomena, as I think the noble Lord, Lord Trefgarne, and the noble Earl, Lord Halsbury, implied.

My Lords, the noble Earl who initiated this debate referred to the attitude of other Governments to UFOs. It is not for me to speak in this House for other Governments. I have however already made mention of the United States study in 1968 and I understand that nothing has happened since that time to cause the United States authorities to change their

only quoted was his statement:

"Careful consideration of the record as it is available to us leads us to conclude that further extensive studies probably cannot be justified in the expectation that science will be advanced thereby."

This report has been much used, as by Lord Strabolgi in this debate, to excuse official reticence on the UFO problem.

views or to warrant further official investigations of UFOs.

The noble Earl also referred to an interview which the then French Minister of Defence, M. Robert Galley gave in 1974 on the subject of UFOs. The noble Earl suggested that M. Galley had said that UFOs were real but that he, the Minister, did not know where they came from. I have read the transcript of M. Galley's broadcast and I also took the trouble to check it in the original French. The essence of what the Minister said was that the phenomena were genuine and were reported by responsible people, but that there were aspects that were difficult to explain. Nowhere did the Minister say that UFOs were real in the sense that they represent alien spacecraft, as suggested by the noble Lord, Lord Rankeillour.

The noble Earl, Lord Kimberley, also said that these had been seen by astronauts. These reports by astronauts were examined in the Colorado Study. The atronauts were required, of course, to report anything unusual perceived on their missions; and indeed many strange phenomena were noted. All the phenomena except three were explained. There was nothing at all to suggest that the unexplained sightings were alien spacecraft, and the limited visibility from the small and smeared windows of a spacecraft did not make visual observation easy.

It has been suggested in this debate that our Government are involved in an alleged conspiracy of silence. I can assure your Lordships that the Government are not engaged in any such conspiracy. In view of what the noble Lord, Lord Gainford, said, I must emphasise that the Ministry of Defence examines any UFO reports received to establish whether they reveal anything of defence interest, but nothing in the reports examined has ever given cause to believe that they represent alien spacecraft. There is nothing to have a conspiracy of silence about. What is more, a visitor from outer space would be one of the great events in history. It would certainly be an event of stupendous importance, but I hesitate to say the greatest event of all in the presence of my old friend the right reverend prelate the Bishop of Norwich, whose moving speech we listened to with much interest.

As the noble Earl, Lord Halsbury, said, scientists are rightly inquisitive people. If there was anything in the stories of UFOs, we would expect the scientific community as a whole to be devoting much offort to studying or to making contact with the supposed aliens; but the idea of a conspiracy of silence by this and other Governments belongs, I suggest, to the world of James Bond.

Then the noble Earl, Lord Kimberley' implied that there was some kind of cover-up. There is no cover-up and no security ban. It is true that when people ask to see the Ministry of Defence UFO files they are told that the papers must remain confidential, but there is a very mundane reason for that. The files contain voluminous correspondence from people, and we cannot divulge the identity of the correspondents. It follows that the files must remain closed under the rules laid down in the Public Record Acts, passed by Parliament, which at present preclude disclosure until 30 years have elapsed since the date of the particular correspondence. The earliest reports the Ministry of Defence hold are dated 1962.

The noble Earl, Lord Clancarty, mentioned the possibility of an intra-governmental study of UFOs. At the United Nations recently, representatives of Grenada made statements about UFOs and proposals for a study. A compromise decision was taken, wherein the General Assembly invited " interested member states " to co-ordinate research " on a national level " and to inform the Secretary-General of their findings. The Secretary-General was requested to transmit the Grenadan statements and other relevant reports to the Committee on the Peaceful Uses of Outer Space. This is not an inter-governmental study, in the sense that the noble Earl, Lord Clancarty, is seeking, but he may be content that Grenada, and perhaps some other countries, may be reporting in an international forum.

Lord KINGS NORTON: My Lords, the word was " intra ", not " inter ".

Lord STRABOLGI: My Lords, I take note of what the noble Lord said. Then it has been suggested, too, in this debate that Her Majesty's Government should set up a study group. I am glad to say that the noble Lord, Lord Trefgarne, and the noble Lord, Lord Gladwyn, both speaking from the Front Benches for the Opposition Parties, did not support this proposal, and certainly Her Majesty's Government do not consider that there is any justification for the expenditure of public money on such a study.

I repeat that I am grateful to the noble Earl, Lord Clancarty, for raising the subject of UFOs, and I am particularly grateful to him for informing me in advance of the points which he proposed to make to your Lordships. However, from all I have said, I am sure that your Lordships will agree that there is no reason for my right honourable friend the Secretary of State for Defence to make a broadcast interview about UFOs, as the noble Earl, Lord Clancarty, suggested. As for telling the public the truth about UFOs, the truth is simple. There really are many strange phenomena in the sky, and these are invariably reported by rational people. But there is a wide range of natural explanations to account for such phenomena. There is nothing to suggest to Her Majesty's Government that such phenomena are alien space craft.

Viscount BARRINGTON: My Lords, may I ask a question? I did rise to ask it when the noble Lord, Lord Strabolgi, rose. I was going to ask it of the noble Earl, Lord Halsbury, but I think it would be more courteous to ask it of the noble Lord, Lord Strabolgi. The subject of this debate is " objects ", and in the expert speech—with almost all of which I agreed —of the noble Earl, Lord Halsbury, he mentioned that scientists, as scientists, are dealing only with material objects. I have to be careful here, as a non-scientist who minds his p's and q's, and who hardly knows a quasar from a pulsar, but is a black hole a material object?

Lord STRABOLGI: My Lords, I should not at all like to follow the noble

Viscount down that avenue. I do not think that even scientists or astronomers know what black holes are. I may say that, in a way, I think it is a pity that the noble Viscount did not take part in the debate.

10.34 p.m.

The Earl of CLANCARTY: My Lords, I should like to thank the noble Lord, Lord Strabolgi, for his assurances and for the information which he has given us. I am sorry that we are not to be able to listen to, or see, his right honourable friend the Secretary of State for Defence, giving a television interview about UFOs. There are just one or two very small points, before I end this debate. We have talked about the umpteen light years that some of these planets and stars are away from us. But we are looking at it from our own standpoint, because we started to fly only in 1903, when the Wright brothers took off. Now we have got Concorde, so we consider ourselves to be rather good. But we say that we cannot go right out into space because of all this distance in light years. Let us suppose, however, as has been suggested, that there are billions of planets with civilisations thousands of years old. Is it not possible that they could come here, after all that time, almost instantaneously? It is just a thought.

A propos of that, I should like to bring to the attention of your Lordships a famous scientist and astronomer, our own Sir Fred Hoyle. Some years ago he wrote a book called *Of Men and*

Galacies. He wrote a passage in that book which I was allowed to quote in one of mine. It read:

" You are all familiar with an ordinary telephone directory. If you want to speak to someone, you look up his number and you dial the appropriate code. My speculation "—

this is Sir Fred Hoyle speaking—

" is that a similar situation exists and has existed for billions of years in the galaxy. My speculation is that an interchange of messages is going on on a vast scale all the time and that we are as unaware of it as a pygmy in the African forests is unaware of the radio messages that flash at the speed of light round the earth. My guess is that there might be a million or more subscribers to the galactic directory. Our problem is to get our name into that directory ".

I think that noble Lords will agree that there is a man of vision. Nothing is impossible in this world or in this universe. It is just that the seemingly impossible takes a little time to come about.

My Lords, we have had an interesting discussion this evening. I should like to thank the right reverend Prelate the Bishop of Norwich and all noble Lords who have taken part in this debate for their wonderful contributions. I should also like to congratulate the noble Viscount, Lord Oxfuird, upon his splendid maiden speech. May I also thank all other noble Lords for their rapt and riveted attention. I beg leave to withdraw the Motion for Papers.

Motion for Papers, by leave, withdrawn.

Afterword.

I had the pleasure of introducing what amounted to a really interesting and historic, full scale, three hour Debate in the House of Lords on January 18, 1979, about Unidentified Flying Objects (UFOs).

During the course of my introductory speech I suggested that because of the growing importance of the subject and the large increase of UFO sightings on a world-wide scale, the subject of the UFOs should be kept in front of Parliament from then onwards, and that one way to do this was to form a House of Lords All Party UFO Study Group. We already have a House of Lords All Party Defence Study Group under the able Chairmanship of 94 year old Lord Shinwell. Incidentally, the Earl of Kimberley who made a most splendid speech supporting me in the Debate about UFOs is Honorary Secretary of the House of Lords Defence Study Group.

In the ensuing days after the Debate many of my colleagues in the House of Lords indicated to me their wish to join such a group.

So we now have got started. At the time of writing we have had two meetings of the Group. The first was held on Tuesday, June 19, 1979, and was a formal one to elect officers, discuss aims and possible guest speakers from both the United Kingdom and abroad.

At our second meeting held on Tuesday, July 10, 1979, we had as our first guest speaker, Mr. Charles Bowen, Editor of *Flying Saucer Review*. FSR, as it is affectionately called, is probably the most prestigious UFO magazine in the world. It is now in its 25th year of publication, and Mr. Bowen has been ably editing it for almost 15 years. A few months ago I got the magazine accepted by the House of Lords Library.

Mr. Bowen gave a most interesting talk which ranged over many UFO sightings and landing reports across the world.

We plan to have a continuous number of guest speakers from all parts of the world. Invitations have gone out to a number of prominent ufologists and the response has been very good. Indeed, due to some press publicity about the new Group, I have had cables from people in the United States offering to address the newly formed Group! So, I am sure that we will not be short of speakers and that we will have some very interesting meetings in the days to come.

The UFO subject has in the last year or so become one that millions of people throughout the world are now much more interested in than before, and so it is only right that our House of Lords should take a part in trying to understand, discuss and evaluate the phenomena.

The UFO Debate was very successful but is now in the past. The UFO situation will now be kept alive in Parliament by the House of Lords All Party Study Group. I should add that members of what we call 'the other place' — that is, the House of Commons — will be most welcome to attend our meetings.

Clancarty.